Personal Radio Service

Part 95

Kent Hertz

The author believes, to the best of his knowledge, that the information provide in this book is correct at the time of this writing.

DISCLAIMER AND/OR LEGAL NOTICES:

Table of Contents

Title 47: Telecommunication

PART 95—PERSONAL RADIO SERVICES

Contents
Subpart A—General Mobile Radio Service (GMRS)

Subpart B—Family Radio Service (FRS)

GENERAL PROVISIONS

§95.193 (FRS Rule 3) Types of communications.
§95.194 (FRS Rule 4) FRS units.
Subpart C—Radio Control (R/C) Radio Service

GENERAL PROVISIONS

§95.201 (R/C Rule 1) What is the Radio Control (R/C) Radio Service?
§95.202 (R/C Rule 2) How do I use these rules?
§95.203 (R/C Rule 3) Am I eligible to operate an R/C station?
§95.204 (R/C Rule 4) Do I need a license?
§95.205 (R/C Rule 5) Where may I operate my R/C station?
§95.206 (R/C Rule 6) Are there any special restrictions on the location of my R/C station?
HOW TO OPERATE AN R/C STATION

§95.207 (R/C Rule 7) On what channels may I operate?
§95.208 (R/C Rule 8) How high may I put my antenna?
§95.209 (R/C Rule 9) What equipment may I use at my R/C station?
§95.210 (R/C Rule 10) How much power may I use?
§95.211 (R/C Rule 11) What communications may be transmitted?
§95.212 (R/C Rule 12) What communications are prohibited?
§95.213 (R/C Rule 13) May I be paid to use my R/C station?
§95.214 (R/C Rule 14) Who is responsible for R/C communications I make?
§95.215 (R/C Rule 15) Do I have to limit the length of my communications?
§95.216 (R/C Rule 16) Do I identify my R/C communications?
§95.217 (R/C Rule 17) May I operate my R/C station transmitter by remote control?
OTHER THINGS YOU NEED TO KNOW

§95.218 (R/C Rule 18) What are the penalties for violating these rules?
§95.219 (R/C Rule 19) How do I answer correspondence from the FCC?
§95.220 (R/C Rules 20) What must I do if the FCC tells me that my R/C station is causing interference?
§95.221 (R/C Rule 21) How do I have my R/C transmitter serviced?
§95.222 (R/C Rule 22) May I make any changes to my R/C station transmitter?
§95.223 (R/C Rule 23) Do I have to make my R/C station available for inspection?
§95.224 (R/C Rule 24) What are my station records?
§95.225 (R/C Rule 25) How do I contact the FCC?
Subpart D—Citizens Band (CB) Radio Service

GENERAL PROVISIONS

§95.401 (CB Rule 1) What are the Citizens Band Radio Services?
§95.402 (CB Rule 2) How do I use these rules?
§95.403 (CB Rule 3) Am I eligible to operate a CB station?
§95.404 (CB Rule 4) Do I need a license?

2

Subpart I—Medical Device Radio communication Service (MedRadio)

Subpart J—Multi-Use Radio Service (MURS)

GENERAL PROVISIONS

Subpart K—Personal Locator Beacons (PLB)

Subpart L—Dedicated Short-Range Communications Service On-Board Units (DSRCS-OBUs)

AUTHORITY: Secs. 4, 303, 48 Stat. 1066, 1082, as amended; 47 U.S.C. 154, 303.

6

EDITORIAL NOTE: Nomenclature changes to part 95 appear at 63 FR 54077, Oct. 8, 1998.

Subpart A—General Mobile Radio Service (GMRS)

SOURCE: 48 FR 35237, Aug. 3, 1983, unless otherwise noted.

§95.1 The General Mobile Radio Service (GMRS).

(a) The *GMRS* is a land mobile radio service available to persons for short-distance two-way communications to facilitate the activities of licensees and their immediate family members. Each licensee manages a system consisting of one or more stations.

(b) The 218-219 MHz Service is a two-way radio service authorized for system licensees to provide communication service to subscribers in a specific service area. The rules for this service are contained in subpart F of this part.

[48 FR 35237, Aug. 3, 1983, as amended at 50 FR 7345, Feb. 22, 1985; 53 FR 47714, Nov. 25, 1988; 57 FR 8275, Mar. 9, 1992; 62 FR 23163, Apr. 29, 1997; 64 FR 59659, Nov. 3, 1999]

§95.3 License required.

Before any station transmits on any channel authorized in the GMRS from any *point* (a geographical location) within or over the territorial limits of any area where radio services are regulated by the FCC, the responsible party must obtain a *license* (a written authorization from the FCC for a GMRS system).

[53 FR 47714, Nov. 25, 1988]

§95.5 Licensee eligibility.

(a) An *individual* (one man or one woman) is eligible to obtain, renew, and have modified a GMRS system license if that

7

individual is 18 years of age or older and is not a representative of a foreign government.

(b) A *non-individual* (an entity other than an individual) is ineligible to obtain a new GMRS system license or make a major modification to an existing GMRS system license (*see* §1.929 of this chapter).

(c) A GMRS system licensed to a non-individual before July 31, 1987, is eligible to renew that license and all subsequent licenses based upon it if:

(1) The non-individual is a partnership and each partner is 18 years of age or older; a corporation; an association; a state, territorial, or local government unit; or a legal entity;

(2) The non-individual is not a foreign government; a representative of a foreign government; or a federal government agency; and

(3) The licensee has not been granted a major modification to its GMRS system.

[64 FR 53241, Oct. 1, 1999]

§95.7 Channel sharing.

(a) Channels or channel pairs (one 462 MHz frequency listed in §95.29(a) of this part and one 467 MHz frequency listed in §95.29(b) of this part) are available to GMRS systems only on a shared basis and will not be assigned for the exclusive use of any licensee. All station operators and GMRS system licensees must cooperate in the selection and use of channels to reduce interference and to make the most effective use of the facilities.

(b) Licensees of GMRS systems suffering or causing harmful interference are expected to cooperate and resolve this problem by mutually satisfactory arrangements. If the licensees are unable to do so, the FCC may impose restrictions including specifying the transmitter power, antenna height, or area or hours of operation of the stations concerned. Further, the use of

Personal Radio Service

any frequency at a given geographical location may be denied when, in the judgment of the FCC, its use in that location is not in the public interest; the use of any channel or channel pair may be restricted as to specified geographical areas, maximum power, or other operating conditions.

[48 FR 35237, Aug. 3, 1983, as amended at 53 FR 47715, Nov. 25, 1988; 63 FR 68974, Dec. 14, 1998; 64 FR 53241, Oct. 1, 1999]

§95.21 GMRS system description.

A *GMRS system* is one or more transmitting units used by station operators to communicate messages. A GMRS system is comprised of:

(a) One or more station operators;

(b) One mobile station consisting of one or more mobile units (see §95.23 of this part);

(c) One or more land stations (optional);

(d) Paging receivers (optional); and

(e) Fixed stations (optional).

[63 FR 68974, Dec. 14, 1998]

§95.23 Mobile station description.

(a) A *mobile station* is one or more units which transmit while moving or during temporary stops at unspecified points.

(b) A mobile station unit may transmit from any point within or over any areas where radio services are regulated by the FCC *except* where additional considerations apply.

(c) A mobile station unit may transmit from an aircraft or ship, with the captain's permission, which is:

9

(1) Within or over any area where radio services are regulated by the FCC *except* where additional restrictions apply; and

(2) On or over international waters, if the unit is transmitting from an aircraft or ship of United States registry.

[48 FR 35237, Aug. 3, 1983, as amended at 49 FR 4003, Feb. 1, 1984; 63 FR 68974, Dec. 14, 1998]

§95.25 Land station description.

(a) A *land station* is a unit which transmits from a specific address as determined by the licensee.

(1) An exact point as shown on the license; or

(2) An unspecified point within an *operating area* (an area within a circle centered on a point chosen by the applicant) as shown on the license, for a *temporary period* (one year or less).

(b) The point from which every land station transmits must be within an area where radio services are regulated by the FCC.

(c) [Reserved]

(d) A *small control station* is any control station which:

(1) Has an antenna no more than 6.1 meters (20 feet) above the ground or above the building or tree on which it is mounted (see §95.51); and

(2) *Is:* (i) South of Line A or west of Line C; or

(ii) North of Line A or east of Line C, and the station transmits with no more than 5 watts *ERP* (effective radiated power).

(e) A *small base station* is any base station that:

10

(1) Has an antenna no more than 6.1 meters (20 feet) above the ground or above the building or tree on which it is mounted (see §95.51); and

(2) Transmits with no more than 5 watts ERP.

(f) Each base station and each control station with an antenna height greater than 6.1 meters (20 feet) must be separately identified on Form 605. *See* §§95.25 (d) and (e) and 95.51 of this part.

[48 FR 35237, Aug. 3, 1983, as amended at 53 FR 47715, Nov. 25, 1988; 53 FR 51625, Dec. 22, 1988; 63 FR 68974, Dec. 14, 1998]

§95.27 Paging receiver description.

A *paging receiver* is a unit capable of receiving the radio signals from a base station for the bearer to hear a *page* (someone's name or other identifier said in order to find, summon or notify him/her) spoken by the base station operator.

§95.29 Channels available.

(a) For a base station, fixed station, mobile station, or repeater station (a GMRS station that simultaneously retransmits the transmission of another GMRS station on a different channel or channels), the licensee of the GMRS system must select the transmitting channels or channel pairs (*see* §95.7(a) of this part) for the stations in the GMRS system from the following 462 MHz channels:

462.5500, 462.5750, 462.6000, 462.6250, 462.6500, 462.6750, 462.7000 and 462.7250.

(b) For a mobile station, control station, or fixed station operated in the duplex mode, the following 467 MHz channels may be used only to transmit communications through a repeater station and for remotely controlling a repeater station. The licensee of the GMRS system must select the transmitting channels or channel pairs (*see* §95.7(a) of this part) for the stations operated in the duplex mode, from the following 467 MHz channels:

467.5500, 467.5750, 467.6000, 467.6250, 467.6500, 467.6750, 467.7000 and 467.7250.

(c)-(e) [Reserved]

(f) Except for a GMRS system licensed to a non-individual, a mobile station or a small base station operating in the simplex mode may transmit on the following 462 MHz interstitial channels:

462.5625, 462.5875, 462.6125, 462,6375, 462.6625, 462.6875 and 462.7125.

These channels may be used only under the following conditions:

(1) Only voice type emissions may be transmitted;

(2) The station does not transmit one-way pages; and

(3) The station transmits with no more than 5 watts ERP.

(g) Fixed stations in GMRS systems authorized before March 18, 1968, located 160 kilometers (100 miles) or more from the geographic center of urbanized areas f 200,000 or more population as defined in the U.S. Census of Population, 1960, Vol. 1, Table 23, page 50 that were authorized to transmit on channels other than those listed in this section may continue to transmit on their originally assigned channels provided that they cause no interference to the operation of stations in any of the part 90 private land mobile radio services.

[53 FR 47715, Nov. 25, 1988, as amended at 63 FR 68974, Dec. 14, 1998; 64 FR 53241, Oct. 1, 1999]

§95.33 Cooperative use of radio stations in the GMRS.

(a) *Licensees* (a licensee is the entity to which the license is issued) of radio stations in the GMRS may share the use of their stations with other entities eligible in the GMRS, subject to the following conditions and limitations.

(1) The station to be shared must be individually owned by the licensee, jointly owned by the participants and the licensee, leased individually by the licensee, or leased jointly by the participants and the licensee.

(2) The licensee must maintain access to and control over all stations authorized under its license.

(3) A station may be shared only:

(i) Without charge;

(ii) On a non-profit basis, with contributions to capital and operating expenses including the cost of mobile stations and paging receivers prorated equitably among all participants; or

(iii) On a reciprocal basis, i.e., use of one licensee's stations for the use of another licensee's stations without charge for either capital or operating expenses.

(4) All sharing arrangements must be conducted in accordance with a written agreement to be kept as part of the station records.

(b) [Reserved]

[48 FR 35237, Aug. 3, 1983, as amended at 63 FR 68975, Dec. 14, 1998]

§95.45 Considerations on Department of Defense land and in other circumstances.

(a) The Department of Defense may impose additional restrictions on a station transmitting on its land. (Before placing a station at such a point, a licensee should consult with the commanding officer in charge of the land.)

(b) Additional restrictions may apply when a land station in a GMRS system is located near FCC field offices, near United States borders, in quiet zones, or when it may have a significant impact upon the environment. *See* §§1.923 and 1.924 of this chapter.

[63 FR 68975, Dec. 14, 1998]

§95.51 Antenna height.

(a) Certain antenna structures used in a GMRS system and that are more than 60.96 m (200 ft) in height, or are located near or at a public-use airport must be notified to the FAA and registered with the Commission as required by part 17 of this chapter.

(b) The antenna for a small base station or for a small control station must not be more than 6.1 meters (20 feet) above the ground or above the building or tree on which it is mounted.

[63 FR 68975, Dec. 14, 1998]

§95.101 What the license authorizes.

(a) A GMRS license authorizes a GMRS station to transmit messages to other GMRS stations at any geographical location within or over the territorial limits of any area where radio services are regulated by the FCC. These points are listed in Appendix A.

(b) The license does not authorize operation as a common carrier or communication of messages for pay.

(c) If the licensee is a corporation and the license so indicates, it may use its GMRS system to furnish non-profit radio communication service to its parent corporation, to another subsidiary of the same parent, or to its own subsidiary. Such use is not subject to the cooperative use provisions of §95.33.

(d) For non-individual licensees, the license together with the system specifications for that license as maintained by the

14

Commission represent the non-individual licensees' maximum authorized system.

[48 FR 35237, Aug. 3, 1983, as amended at 63 FR 68975, Dec. 14, 1998; 64 FR 53242, Oct. 1, 1999]

§95.103 Licensee duties.

The licensee is responsible for the proper operation of the GMRS system at all times. The licensee is also responsible for the appointment of a station operator.

[63 FR 68975, Dec. 14, 1998]

EDITORIAL NOTE: At 64 FR 53242, Oct. 1, 1999, §95.103 was amended by revising paragraphs (a) and (b), effective Nov. 30, 1999. However, §95.103, as revised at 63 FR 68975, Dec. 14, 1998, effective Feb. 12, 1999, does not contain paragraphs (a) and (b), and the revisions could not be made. For the convenience of the user, the revised text is set forth as follows:

§95.103 Licensee duties.

(a) The licensee is responsible for the proper operation of the GMRS system at all times. The licensee is also responsible for the appointment of a station operator.

(b) The licensee may limit the use of repeater to only certain user stations.

§95.105 License term.

A license for a GMRS system is usually issued for a 5-year term.

[63 FR 68975, Dec. 14, 1998]

15

§95.115 Station inspection.

If an authorized FCC representative requests to inspect any station in a GMRS system, the licensee or station operator must make the station available. If an authorized FCC representative requests to inspect the GMRS system records, the licensee must make them available.

[48 FR 35237, Aug. 3, 1983, as amended at 63 FR 68975, Dec. 14, 1998]

§95.117 Where to contact the FCC.

Additional GMRS information may be obtained from any of the following sources:

(a) FCC National Call Center at 1-888-225-5322.

(b) FCC World Wide Web homepage: *http://www.fcc.gov/wtb/prs*.

(c) In writing, to the FCC, Attention: GMRS, 1270 Fairfield Road, Gettysburg, PA 17325-7245.

[63 FR 68975, Dec. 14, 1998]

§95.119 Station identification.

(a) Except as provided in paragraph (e), every GMRS station must transmit a station identification:

(1) Following the transmission of communications or a series of communications; and

(2) Every 15 minutes during a long transmission.

(b) The station identification is the call sign assigned to the GMRS station or system.

(c) A unit number may be included after the call sign in the identification.

16

(d) The station identification must be transmitted in:

(1) Voice in the English language; or

(2) International Morse code telegraphy.

(e) A station need not identify its transmissions if it automatically retransmits communications from another station which are properly identified.

[48 FR 35237, Aug. 3, 1983, as amended at 63 FR 68975, Dec. 14, 1998]

§95.129 Station equipment.

Every station in a GMRS system must use transmitters the FCC has certificated for use in the GMRS. Write to any FCC Field Office to find out if a particular transmitter has been certificated for the GMRS. All station equipment in a GMRS system must comply with the technical rules in part 95.

[63 FR 68975, Dec. 14, 1998]

§95.135 Maximum authorized transmitting power.

(a) No station may transmit with more than 50 watts output power.

(b) [Reserved]

(c) A small control station at a point north of Line A or east of Line C must transmit with no more than 5 watts ERP.

(d) A fixed station must transmit with no more than 15 watts output power.

(e) A small base station must transmit with no more than 5 watts ERP.

[48 FR 35237, Aug. 3, 1983, as amended at 53 FR 47717, Nov. 25, 1988; 63 FR 68975, Dec. 14, 1998]

§95.139 Adding a small base station or a small control station.

(a) Except for a GMRS system licensed to a non-individual, one or more small base stations or a small control station may be added to a GMRS system at any point where radio services are regulated by the FCC.

(b) Non-individual licensees may not add any small base station or small control stations to their GMRS systems.

[53 FR 47717, Nov. 25, 1988, as amended at 63 FR 68976, Dec. 14, 1998]

§95.141 Interconnection prohibited.

No station in a GMRS system may be interconnected to the public switched telephone network except as and in accordance with the requirements and restrictions applied to a wireline control link (see §95.127).

[53 FR 47717, Nov. 25, 1988]

§95.143 Managing a GMRS system in an emergency.

(a) The stations in a GMRS system must cease transmitting when the station operator of any station on the same channel is communicating an *emergency message* (concerning the immediate protection of property or the safety of someone's life).

(b) If necessary to communicate an emergency message from a station in a GMRS system, the licensee may permit:

(1) Anyone to be the station operator (see §95.179); and

(2) The station operator to communicate the emergency message to any radio station.

§95.171 Station operator duties.

When a GMRS station is transmitting, it must have a station operator. The station operator must be at the control point for that station. The same person may be the operator for more than one station at the same time. The station operator communicates messages and controls the station. The station operator must also cooperate in *sharing* each channel with station operators of other stations.

[63 FR 68976, Dec. 14, 1998]

§95.179 Individuals who may be station operators.

(a) An individual GMRS system licensee may permit immediate family members to be station operators in his or her GMRS system. Immediate family members are the:

(1) Licensee;

(2) Licensee's spouse;

(3) Licensee's children, grandchildren, stepchildren;

(4) Licensee's parents, grandparents, stepparents;

(5) Licensee's brothers, sisters;

(6) Licensee's aunts, uncles, nieces, nephews; and

(7) Licensee's in-laws.

(b) Only the following persons may be permitted to operate under the authority of a GMRS system licensed to a non-individual:

(1) If the GMRS system licensee is:	These persons may be station operators:
(i) A partnership	Licensee's partners and employees.
(ii) A corporation	Licensee's officers, directors, members and employees.
(iii) An association	Licensee's members and employees.
(iv) A governmental unit	Licensee's employees.

(2) These persons may only communicate messages about the licensee's business activities. Employees of the licensee may communicate messages while acting within the scope of their employment, and only about the licensee's business activities.

(c) The licensee may permit a telephone answering service employee to be a station operator if:

(1) That employee only communicates messages received for the licensee to the licensee;

(2) The station equipment at the telephone answering point is not shared in any other GMRS system; and

(3) The station at the telephone answering service point is not interconnected to the public switched telephone network.

(d) The station operator of a GMRS system licensed to an individual may be a station operator in any other GMRS system if he/she has permission from the licensee of the other GMRS system.

(e) The provisions of §95.33 regarding cooperative use do not apply to or govern the authority of a GMRS licensee to designate station operators in accordance with the provisions of this section.

[48 FR 35237, Aug. 3, 1983, as amended at 53 FR 47717, Nov. 25, 1988; 53 FR 51625, Dec. 22, 1988; 63 FR 68976, Dec. 14, 1998]

§95.181 Permissible communications.

(a) A station operator for an individual who is licensed in the GMRS (other than an employee of that individual) may communicate two-way voice messages concerning the licensee's personal or business activities (see §95.179).

(b) [Reserved]

(c) A station operator for any entity other than an individual licensed in the GMRS may communicate two-way voice messages concerning the licensee's business activities (see §95.179). An employee for an entity other than an individual licensed in the GMRS may, as a station operator, communicate two-way voice messages while acting within the scope of his/her employment.

(d) A station operator for any GMRS licensee may communicate two-way voice messages concerning:

(1) Emergencies (see §95.143);

(2) Rendering assistance to a motorist; and

(3) Civil defense drills, if the responsible agency requests assistance.

(e) All messages must be in *plain language* (without codes or hidden meanings). They may be in a foreign language, except for call signs (see §95.119).

(f) A station operator may communicate tone messages for purposes of identification or transmitter control in a control link.

(g) A station operator may communicate a selective calling tone or tone operated squelch only in conjunction with a voice communication. If the tone is *subaudible* (300 Hertz or less) it may be communicated during the entire voice message. If the tone is *audible* (more than 300 Hertz) it may be communicated for no more than 15 seconds at a time.

(h) A station operator may communicate a one-way voice page to a paging receiver. A selective calling tone or tone operated squelch may be used in conjunction with a voice page, as prescribed in paragraph (g) of this section. A station operator may not communicate a *tone-only page* (tones communicated in order to find, summon or notify someone).

[48 FR 35237, Aug. 3, 1983, as amended at 49 FR 4003, Feb. 1, 1984; 56 FR 13289, Apr. 1, 1991; 63 FR 68976, Dec. 14, 1998]

§95.183 Prohibited communications.

(a) A station operator must not communicate:

(1) Messages for hire, whether the remuneration received is direct or indirect;

(2) Messages in connection with any activity which is against Federal, State, or local law;

(3) False or deceptive messages;

(4) Coded messages or messages with hidden meanings ("10 codes" are permissible);

(5) Intentional interference;

(6) Music, whistling, sound effects or material to amuse or entertain;

(7) Obscene, profane or indecent words, language or meaning;

(8) Advertisements or offers for the sale of goods or services;

(9) Advertisements for a political candidate or political campaign (messages about the campaign business may be communicated);

(10) International distress signals, such as the word "Mayday" (except when on a ship, aircraft or other vehicle in immediate danger to ask for help);

(11) Programs (live or delayed) intended for radio or television station broadcast;

(12) Messages which are both conveyed by a wireline control link and transmitted by a GMRS station;

(13) Messages (except emergency messages) to any station in the Amateur Radio Service, to any unauthorized station, or to any foreign station;

(14) Continuous or uninterrupted transmissions, except for communications involving the immediate safety of life or property;

(15) Messages for public address systems.

(b) A station operator in a GMRS system licensed to a telephone answering service must not transmit any communications to customers of the telephone answering service.

[63 FR 68976, Dec. 14, 1998]

Appendix A to Subpart A of Part 95—Locations Where GMRS Is Regulated by the FCC

In ITU Region 2, the GMRS is regulated by the Commission within the territorial limits of the 50 United States, District of Columbia, Caribbean Insular areas (Commonwealth of Puerto Rico, United States Virgin Islands (50 islets and cays) and Navassa Island), and Johnston Island (Islets East, Johnston, North and Sand) and Midway Island (Islets Eastern and Sand) in the Pacific Insular areas.

In ITU Region 3, the GMRS is regulated by the Commission within the Pacific Insular territorial limits of American Samoa (seven islands), Baker Island, Commonwealth of Northern Mariana Islands, Guam Island, Howland Island, Jarvis Island, Kingman Reef, Palmyra Island (more than 50 islets), and Wake Island (Islets Peale, Wake and Wilkes).

[63 FR 68976, Dec. 14, 1998]

Subpart B—Family Radio Service (FRS)

SOURCE: 61 FR 28768, June 6, 1996, unless otherwise noted.

GENERAL PROVISIONS

§95.191 (FRS Rule 1) Eligibility and responsibility.

(a) Unless you are a representative of a foreign government, you are authorized by this rule to operate an FCC certified FRS unit in accordance with the rules in this subpart. No license will be issued.

(b) You are responsible for all communications that you make with the FRS unit. You must share each channel with other users. No channel is available for the private or exclusive use of any user.

§95.192 (FRS Rule 2) Authorized locations.

(a) Provided that you comply with these rules, you are authorized to operate an FRS unit:

(1) Within or over any area of the world where radio services are regulated by the FCC (this area includes the fifty United States and the District of Columbia, the Commonwealth of Puerto Rico, the United States Virgin Islands (50 islets and cays), American Samoa (seven islands), the Commonwealth of Northern Marianna Islands, and Guam Island);

(2) Within or over any other area of the world, except within or over the territorial limits of areas where radio services are regulated by an agency of the United States other than the FCC or any foreign government (you are subject to its rules);

(3) Aboard any vessel or aircraft registered in the United States, with the permission of the captain, that is within or over any area of the world where radio services are regulated by the FCC or upon or over international waters;

(4) or; Aboard any unregistered vessel or aircraft owned or operated by a United States citizen or company that is within or over any area of the world where radio services are regulated by the FCC or upon or over international waters.

(5) You must operate the FRS unit only according to any applicable treaty to which the United States is a party. The FCC will make public notice of any such conditions.

(b)-(c) [Reserved]

(d) Anyone intending to operate an FRS unit on the islands of Puerto Rico, Desecheo, Mona, Vieques, and Culebra in a manner that could pose an interference threat to the Arecibo Observatory, shall notify the Interference Office, Arecibo Observatory, HC3 Box 53995, Arecibo, Puerto Rico 00612, in writing or electronically, of the location of the unit. Operators may wish to consult interference guidelines, which will be provided by Cornell University. Operators who choose to transmit information electronically should e-mail to: *prcz@naic.edu*.

(1) The notification to the Interference Office, Arecibo Observatory shall be made 45 days prior to commencing operation of the unit. The notification shall state the geographical coordinates of the unit.

(2) After receipt of such notifications, the Commission will allow the Arecibo Observatory a period of 20 days for comments or objections. The operator will be required to make reasonable efforts in order to resolve or mitigate any potential interference problem with the Arecibo Observatory. If the Commission determines that an operator has satisfied its responsibility to make reasonable efforts to protect the Observatory from interference, the unit may be allowed to operate.

[61 FR 28768, June 6, 1996, as amended at 62 FR 55535, Oct. 27, 1997; 63 FR 68976, Dec. 14, 1998; 70 FR 31374, June 1, 2005]

§95.193 (FRS Rule 3) Types of communications.

(a) You may use an FRS unit to conduct two-way voice communications with another person. You may use an FRS unit to transmit one-way voice or non-voice communications only to establish communications with another person, send an emergency message, provide traveler assistance, provide location information, transmit a brief text message, make a voice page, or to conduct a brief test.

(b) *Non-voice communications.* (1) The FRS unit may transmit tones to make contact or to continue communications with a particular FRS unit. If the tone is audible (more than 300 Hertz), it must be transmitted continuously no longer than 15 seconds at one time. If the tone is subaudible (300 Hertz or less), it may be transmitted continuously only while you are talking.

(2) The FRS unit may transmit digital data containing location information, or requesting location information from one or more other FRS units, or containing a brief text message to another specific FRS unit. Digital data transmissions must be initiated by a manual action or command of a user, except that an FRS unit receiving an interrogation request may automatically respond with its location. Digital data transmissions shall not exceed one second, and shall be limited to no more than one digital transmission within a thirty-second period, except that an FRS unit may automatically respond to more than one interrogation request received within a thirty-second period.

(c) You must not use an FRS unit in connection with any activity which is against federal, state or local law.

(d) You must, at all times and on all channels, give priority to emergency communication messages concerning the immediate safety of life or the immediate protection of property.

(e) No FRS unit may be interconnected to the public switched network.

[61 FR 28768, June 6, 1996, as amended at 68 FR 9901, Mar. 3, 2003]

§95.194 (FRS Rule 4) FRS units.

(a) You may only use an FCC certified FRS unit. (You can identify an FCC certified FRS unit by the label placed on it by the manufacturer.)

(b) You must not make, or have made, any internal modification to an FRS unit. Any internal modification cancels the FCC certification and voids your authority to operate the unit in the FRS.

(c) You may not attach any antenna, power amplifier, or other apparatus to an FRS unit that has not been FCC certified as part of that FRS unit. There are no exceptions to this rule and attaching any such apparatus to a FRS unit cancels the FCC certification and voids everyone's authority to operate the unit in the FRS.

(d) FRS units are prohibited from transmitting data in store-and-forward packet operation mode.

[61 FR 28768, June 6, 1996, as amended at 68 FR 9901, Mar. 3, 2003]

Subpart C—Radio Control (R/C) Radio Service

SOURCE: 48 FR 24890, June 3, 1983, unless otherwise noted.

GENERAL PROVISIONS

§95.201 (R/C Rule 1) What is the Radio Control (R/C) Radio Service?

The R/C Service is a private, one-way, short distance non-voice communications service for the operation of devices at remote locations.

§95.202 (R/C Rule 2) How do I use these rules?

(a) You must comply with rules (see R/C Rule 18, §95.218, for the penalties for violations) when you operate a station in the R/C service from:

(1) Within or over the territorial limits of places where radio services are regulated by the FCC (see R/C Rule 5, §95.205);

(2) Aboard any vessel or aircraft registered in the United States; or

(3) Aboard any unregistered vessel or aircraft owned or operated by a United States citizen or company.

(b) Your R/C station must comply with technical rules found in subpart E of part 95.

(c) Where the rules use the word "you", "you" means a person operating an R/C station.

(d) Where the rules use the word "person," the rules are concerned with an individual, a corporation, a partnership, an association, a joint stock company, a trust, a state, territorial or local government unit, or other legal entity.

(e) Where the rules use the term "FCC," that means the Federal Communications Commission.

(f) Where the rules use the term "R/C station," that means a radio station transmitting in the R/C Radio Service.

§95.203 (R/C Rule 3) Am I eligible to operate an R/C station?

You are authorized to operate an R/C station unless:

(a) You are a foreign government, a representative of a foreign government, or a federal government agency; or

(b) The FCC has issued a cease and desist order to you, and the order is still in effect.

§95.204 (R/C Rule 4) Do I need a license?

You do not need an individual license to operate an R/C station. You are authorized by this rule to operate your R/C station in accordance with the rules in this subpart.

§95.205 (R/C Rule 5) Where may I operate my R/C station?

You are authorized to operate your R/C station from:

(a) Within or over any area of the world where radio services are regulated by the FCC. Those areas are within the territorial limits of:

(1) The fifty United States

(2) The District of Columbia

Caribbean Insular areas

(3) Commonwealth of Puerto Rico

(4) Navassa Island

(5) United States Virgin Islands (50 islets and cays)

Pacific Insular areas

(6) American Samoa (seven islands)

(7) Baker Island

(8) Commonwealth of Northern Mariana Islands

(9) Guam Island

(10) Howland Island

(11) Jarvis Island

(12) Johnston Island (Islets East, Johnston, North and Sand)

(13) Kingman Reef

(14) Midway Island (Islets Eastern and Sand)

(15) Palmyra Island (more than 50 islets)

(16) Wake Island (Islets Peale, Wake and Wilkes)

(b) Any other area of the world, except within the territorial limits of areas where radio services are regulated by—

(1) An agency of the United States other than the FCC. (You are subject to its rules.)

(2) Any foreign government. (You are subject to its rules.)

(c) An aircraft or ship, with the permission of the captain, within or over any area of the world where radio services are regulated by the FCC or upon or over international waters. You must operate your R/C station according to any applicable treaty to which the United States is a party.

§95.206 (R/C Rule 6) Are there any special restrictions on the location of my R/C station?

(a) If your R/C station is located on premises controlled by the Department of Defense, you may be required to comply with additional regulations imposed by the commanding officer of the installation.

(b) If your R/C station will be constructed on an environmental sensitive site, or will be operated in such a manner as to raise environmental problems, under §1.1307 of this chapter, you must provide an environmental assessment, as set forth in §1.1311 of this chapter, and undergo environmental review §1.1312 of this chapter, before commencement of construction.

(c) Anyone intending to operate an R/C station on the islands of Puerto Rico, Desecheo, Mona, Vieques, and Culebra in a manner that could pose an interference threat to the Arecibo Observatory shall notify the Interference Office, Arecibo Observatory, HC3 Box 53995, Arecibo, Puerto Rico 00612, in writing or electronically, of the location of the unit. Operators may wish to consult interference guidelines, which will be provided by Cornell University. Operators who choose to transmit information electronically should e-mail to: *prcz@naic.edu.*

(1) The notification to the Interference Office, Arecibo Observatory shall be made 45 days prior to commencing operation of the unit. The notification shall state the geographical coordinates of the unit.

(2) After receipt of such notifications, the Commission will allow the Arecibo Observatory a period of 20 days for comments or objections. The operator will be required to make reasonable efforts in order to resolve or mitigate any potential interference problem with the Arecibo Observatory. If the Commission determines that an operator has satisfied its responsibility to make reasonable efforts to protect the Observatory from interference, the unit may be allowed to operate.

[48 FR 24890, June 3, 1983, as amended at 55 FR 20398, May 16, 1990; 62 FR 55535, Oct. 27, 1997; 70 FR 31374, June 1, 2005]

How To Operate an R/C Station

§95.207 (R/C Rule 7) On what channels may I operate?

(a) Your R/C station may transmit only on the following channels (frequencies):

(1) The following channels may be used to operate any kind of device (any object or apparatus, except an R/C transmitter), including a model aircraft device (any small imitation of an aircraft) or a model surface craft device (any small imitation of a boat, car or vehicle for carrying people or objects, except aircraft): 26.995, 27.045, 27.095, 27.145, 27.195 and 27.255 MHz.

(2) The following channels may only be used to operate a model aircraft device:

MHz

72.01	72.51
72.03	72.53
72.05	72.55
72.07	72.57
72.09	72.59
72.11	72.61
72.13	72.63
72.15	72.65
72.17	72.67
72.19	72.69
72.21	72.71
72.23	72.73
72.25	72.75
72.27	72.77
72.29	72.79
72.31	72.81
72.33	72.83
72.35	72.85

72.37 72.87
72.39 72.89
72.41 72.91
72.43 72.93
72.45 72.95
72.47 72.97
72.49 72.99

(3) The following channels may only be used to operate a model surface craft devices:

MHz

75.41 75.71
75.43 75.73
75.45 75.75
75.47 75.77
75.49 75.79
75.51 75.81
75.53 75.83
75.55 75.85
75.57 75.87
75.59 75.89
75.61 75.91
75.63 75.93
75.65 75.95
75.67 75.97
75.69 75.99

(b) You must share the channels with other R/C stations. You must cooperate in the selection and use of the channels. You must share the Channel 27.255 MHz with stations in other radio services. There is no protection from interference on any of these channels.

(c) Your R/C station may not transmit simultaneously on more than one channel in the 72-76 MHz band when your operation would cause harmful interference to the operation of other R/C stations.

(d) Your R/C station must stop transmitting if it interferes with:

(1) Authorized radio operations in the 72-76 MHz band; or

(2) Television reception on TV Channels 4 or 5.

(e) [Reserved]

(f) Stations in the 26-27 MHz range are not afforded any protection from interference caused by the operation of industrial, scientific of medical devices. Such stations also operate on a shared basis with other stations in the Personal Radio Services.

(g) Stations in the 72-76 MHz range are subject to the condition that interference will not be caused to the remote control of industrial equipment operating on the same or adjacent frequencies or to the reception of television transmissions on Channels 4 and 5. These frequencies are not afforded any protection from interference due to the operation of fixed and mobile stations in other services assigned to the same or adjacent frequencies.

[48 FR 24890, June 3, 1983. Redesignated at 49 FR 6098, Feb. 17, 1984, and amended at 50 FR 37857, Sept. 18, 1985; 52 FR 16263, May 4, 1987; 57 FR 40343, Sept. 3, 1992]

§95.208 (R/C Rule 8) How high may I put my antenna?

(a) *Antenna* means the radiating system (for transmitting, receiving or both) and the structure holding it up (tower, pole or mast). It also means everything else attached to the radiating system and the structure.

(b) If your antenna is mounted on a hand-held portable unit, none of the following limitations apply.

(c) If your antenna is installed at a fixed location, it (whether receiving, transmitting or both) must comply with either one of the following:

(1) The highest point must not be more than 6.10 meters (20 feet) higher than the highest point of the building or tree on which it is mounted; or

(2) The highest point must not be more than 18.3 meters (60 feet) above the ground.

(d) If your R/C station is located near an airport, and if you antenna structure is more than 6.1 meters (20 feet) high, your may have to obey additional restrictions. The highest point of your antenna must not exceed one meter above the airport elevation for every hundred meters of distance from the nearest point of the nearest airport runway. Differences in ground elevation between your antenna and the airport runway may complicate this formula. If your R/C station is near an airport, you may contact the nearest FCC field office for a worksheet to help you figure the maximum allowable height of your antenna. Consult part 17 of the FCC's Rules for more information.

WARNING: Installation and removal of R/C station antennas near power lines is dangerous. For your safety, follow the installation directions included with your antenna.

[48 FR 24890, June 3, 1983, as amended at 48 FR 41416, Sept. 15, 1983]

§95.209 (R/C Rule 9) What equipment may I use at my R/C station?

(a) Your R/C station may transmit only with:

(1) An FCC certificated R/C transmitter (certificated means the FCC has determined that certain radio equipment is capable of meeting recommended standards for operation); or

(2) A non-certificated R/C transmitter on Channels 26.995-27.255 MHz if it complies with the technical standards (see part 95, subpart E).

(3) Use of a transmitter outside of the band 26.955-27.255 MHz which is not certificated voids your authority to operate the station. Use of a transmitter in the band 26.995-27.255 MHz which does not comply with the technical standards voids your authority to operate the station.

(b) You may examine a list of certificated transmitters at any FCC field office.

(c) Your R/C station may transmit with a transmitter assembled from a kit.

(d) You must not make, or have made, any internal modification to a certificated transmitter. (See R/C Rule 22.) Any internal modification to a certificated transmitter cancels the certification, and use of such a transmitter voids your authority to operate the station.

[63 FR 36610, July 7, 1998]

§95.210 (R/C Rule 10) How much power may I use?

(a) Your R/C station transmitter power output must not exceed the following value under any conditions:

Channel	Transmitter power (carrier power) (watts)
27.255 MHz	25
26.995-27.195 MHz	4
72-76 MHz	0.75

(b) Use of a transmitter which has power output in excess of that authorized voids your authority to operate the station.

§95.211 (R/C Rule 11) What communications may be transmitted?

(a) You may only use your R/C station to transmit one-way communications. (One-way communications are transmissions which are not intended to establish communications with another station.)

(b) You may only use your R/C station for the following purposes:

(1) The operator turns on and/or off a device at a remote location (Refer to Diagram 1); or

(2) A sensor at a remote location turns on and/off an indicating device for the operator. (Refer to Diagram 2). Only Channels 26.995 to 27.255 MHz (see R/C Rule 7, §95.207(a)(1)) may be used for this purpose. (A remote location means a place distant from the operator.)

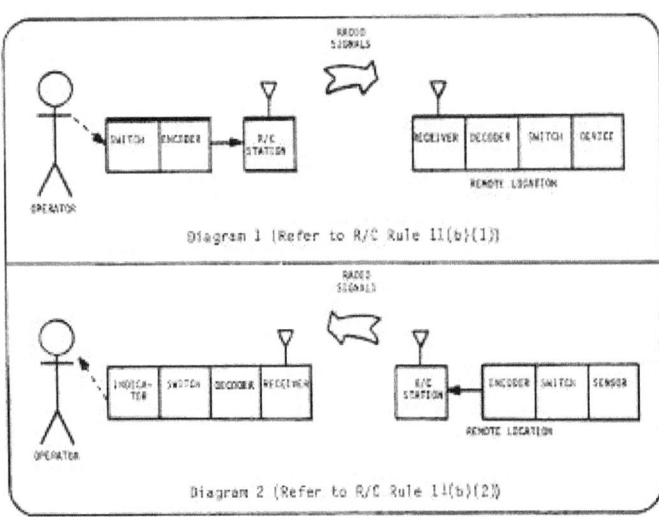

Diagram 1 (Refer to R/C Rule 11(b)(1))

Diagram 2 (Refer to R/C Rule 11(b)(2))

(c) Your R/C station may transmit any appropriate non-voice emission.

[48 FR 24890, June 3, 1983, as amended at 50 FR 37857, Sept. 18, 1985; 57 FR 40343, Sept. 3, 1992]

§95.212 (R/C Rule 12) What communications are prohibited?

You must not use an R/C station—

(a) In connection with any activity which is against federal, state or local law;

(b) To transmit any message other than for operation of devices at remote locations (no voice, telegraphy, etc.);

(c) To intentionally interfere with another station's transmissions;

(d) To operate another R/C transmitter by remote control (See R/C Rule 17, §95.217); or

(e) To transmit two-way communications.

(f) To transmit data. Tone or other signal encoding, however, is not considered to be data when only used either for the purpose of identifying the specific device among multiple devices that the operator intends to turn on/off, or the specific sensor among multiple sensors intended to turn on/off indicating device for the operator.

[48 FR 24890, June 3, 1983, as amended at 54 FR 8336, Feb. 28, 1989; 54 FR 20476, May 11, 1989]

§95.213 (R/C Rule 13) May I be paid to use my R/C station?

(a) You may not accept direct or indirect payment for transmitting with an R/C station.

(b) You may use an R/C station to help you provide a service, and be paid for that service, as long as you are paid only for the service and not for the actual use of the R/C station.

§95.214 (R/C Rule 14) Who is responsible for R/C communications I make?

You are responsible for all communications which are made by you from an R/C station.

§95.215 (R/C Rule 15) Do I have to limit the length of my communications?

(a) You must limit your R/C communications to the minimum practical time.

(b) The only time your R/C communications may be a continuous signal for more than 3 minutes is when operation of the device requires at least one or more changes during each minute of the communications.

(c) Your R/C station may transmit a continuous signal without modulation only if:

(1) You are using it to operate a model aircraft device; and

(2) The presence or absence of the signal operates the device.

(d) If you show that you need a continuous signal to insure the immediate safety of life of property, the FCC may make an exception to the limitations in this rule.

§95.216 (R/C Rule 16) Do I identify my R/C communications?

You need not identify your R/C communications.

§95.217 (R/C Rule 17) May I operate my R/C station transmitter by remote control?

(a) You may not operate an R/C transmitter by radio remote control. (See R/C Rule 12, §95.212.)

(b) You may operate an R/C transmitter by wireline remote control if you obtain specific approval in writing from the FCC. To obtain FCC approval, you must show why you need to operate your station by wireline remote control. If you receive FCC approval, you must keep the approval as part of your station records. *See* R/C Rule 24, §95.224.

(c) Remote control means operation of an R/C transmitter from any place other than the location of the R/C transmitter. Direct mechanical control or direct electrical control by wire from some point on the same premises, craft or vehicles as the R/C transmitter is not considered remote control.

[48 FR 24890, June 3, 1983, as amended at 63 FR 68976, Dec. 14, 1998]

OTHER THINGS YOU NEED TO KNOW

§95.218 (R/C Rule 18) What are the penalties for violating these rules?

(a) If the FCC finds that you have willfully or repeatedly violated the Communications Act or the FCC Rules, you may have to pay as much as $10,000 for each violation, up to a total of $75,000. (See Section 503(b) of the Communications Act.)

(b) If the FCC finds that you have violated any section of the Communications Act or the FCC Rules, you may be ordered to stop whatever action caused the violation. (See section 312(b) of the Communications Act.)

(c) If a federal court finds that you have willfully and knowingly violated any FCC Rule, you may be fined up to $500 for each day you committed the violation. (See section 502 of the Communications Act.)

(d) If a Federal court finds that you have willfully and knowingly violated any provision of the Communications Act, you may be fined up to $10,000, or you may be imprisoned for one year, or both. (See section 501 of the Communications Act.)

[48 FR 24890, June 3, 1983, as amended at 57 FR 40343, Sept. 3, 1992]

§95.219 (R/C Rule 19) How do I answer correspondence from the FCC?

(a) If it appears to the FCC that you have violated the Communications Act or FCC rules, the FCC may send you a discrepancy notice.

(b) Within the time period stated in the notice, you must answer with:

(1) A complete written statement about the apparent discrepancy;

(2) A complete written statement about any action you have taken to correct the apparent violation and to prevent it from happening again; and

(3) The name of the person operating at the time of the apparent violation.

(c) If the FCC send you a letter asking you questions about your R/C radio station or its operation, you must answer each of the questions with a complete written statement within the time period stated in the letter.

(d) You must not shorten your answer by references to other communications or notices.

(e) You must send your answer to the FCC office which sent you the notice.

(f) You must keep a copy of your answer in your station records (see R/C Rule 24, §95.224).

§95.220 (R/C Rules 20) What must I do if the FCC tells me that my R/C station is causing interference?

(a) If the FCC tells you that your R/C station is causing interference for technical reasons, you must follow all instructions in the official FCC notice. (This notice may require you to have technical adjustments made to your equipment.)

(b) You must comply with any restricted hours of R/C station operation which may be included in the official FCC notice.

§95.221 (R/C Rule 21) How do I have my R/C transmitter serviced?

(a) You may adjust an antenna to your R/C transmitter and you may make radio checks. (A radio check means a one-way transmission for a short time in order to test the transmitter.)

(b) You are responsible for the proper operation of the station at all times and are expected to provide for observations, servicing and maintenance as often as may be necessary to ensure proper operation. Each internal repair and each internal adjustment to an FCC certificated R/C transmitter (see R/C Rule 9) must be made in accord with the Technical Regulations (see subpart E). The internal repairs or internal adjustments should be performed by or under the immediate supervision and responsibility of a person certified as technically qualified to perform transmitter maintenance and repair duties in the private land mobile services and fixed services by an organization or committee representative of users in those services.

(c) Except as provided in paragraph (d) of this section, each internal repair and each internal adjustment of an R/C transmitter in which signals are transmitted must be made using a nonradiating ("dummy") antenna.

(d) Brief test signals (signals not longer than one minute during any five minute period) using a radiating antenna may be transmitted in order to:

(1) Adjust a transmitter to an antenna;

(2) Detect or measure radiation of energy other than the intended signal; or

(3) Tune a receiver to your R/C transmitter.

(Secs. 4(i) and 303(r), Communications Act of 1934, as amended, 47 U.S.C. 154(i) and 303(r), and sec. 553 of the Administrative Procedures Act, 5 U.S.C. 553)

[48 FR 24890, June 3, 1983, as amended at 49 FR 20673, May 16, 1984; 63 FR 36610, July 7, 1998]

§95.222 (R/C Rule 22) May I make any changes to my R/C station transmitter?

(a) You must not make or have anyone else make an internal modification to your R/C transmitter.

(b) Internal modification does not include:

(1) Repair or servicing of an R/C station transmitter (see R/C Rule 21, §95.221); or

(2) Changing plug-in modules which were certificated as part of your R/C transmitter.

(c) You must not operate an R/C transmitter which has been modified by anyone in any way, including modification to operate on unauthorized frequencies or with illegal power. (See R/C Rules 9 and 10, §§95.209 and 95.210.)

[48 FR 24894, June 3, 1983, as amended at 63 FR 36610, July 7, 1998]

§95.223 (R/C Rule 23) Do I have to make my R/C station available for inspection?

(a) If an authorized FCC representative requests to inspect your R/C station, you must make your R/C station and records available for inspection.

(b) An R/C station includes all of the radio equipment you use.

§95.224 (R/C Rule 24) What are my station records?

Your station records include the following documents, as applicable:

(a) A copy of each response to an FCC violation notice or an FCC letter. (See R/C Rule 19, §95.219.)

(b) Each written permission received from the FCC. (See R/C Rule 17.)

46

§95.225 (R/C Rule 25) How do I contact the FCC?

(a) FCC National Call Center at 1-888-225-5322.

(b) FCC World Wide Web homepage: *http://www.fcc.gov.*

(c) In writing, to FCC, Attention: R/C, 1270 Fairfield Road, Gettysburg, PA 17325-7245.

[63 FR 68976, Dec. 14, 1998]

Subpart D—Citizens Band (CB) Radio Service

SOURCE: 48 FR 24894, June 3, 1983, unless otherwise noted.

GENERAL PROVISIONS

§95.401 (CB Rule 1) What are the Citizens Band Radio Services?

The Citizens Band Radio Services are:

(a) The Citizens Band (CB) Radio Service—a private, two-way, short-distance voice communications service for personal or business activities of the general public. The CB Radio Service may also be used for voice paging.

(b) The Family Radio Service (FRS)—a private, two-way, very short-distance voice and data communications service for facilitating family and group activities. The rules for this service are contained in subpart B of this part.

(c) The Low Power Radio Service (LPRS)—a private, short-distance communication service providing auditory assistance to persons with disabilities, persons who require language translation, and persons in educational settings, health care assistance to the ill, law enforcement tracking services in cooperation with law enforcement, and point-to-point network control communications for Automated Marine Telecommunications System (AMTS) coast stations licensed under part 80 of this chapter. The rules for this service are listed under subpart G of this part. Two-way voice communications are prohibited.

(d) The Medical Device Radio communication Service (MedRadio)—an ultra-low power radio service, for the transmission of non-voice data for the purpose of facilitating diagnostic and/or therapeutic functions involving implanted and body-worn medical devices. The rules for this service are contained in subpart I of this part.

48

(e) The Wireless Medical Telemetry Service (WMTS)—a private, short distance data communication service for the transmission of patient medical information to a central monitoring location in a hospital or other medical facility. Voice and video communications are prohibited. Waveforms such as electrocardiograms (ECGs) are not considered video. The rules for this service are contained in subpart H of this part.

(f) The Multi-Use Radio Service (MURS)—a private, two-way, short-distance voice or data communications service for personal or business activities of the general public. The rules for this service are contained in subpart J of this part.

(g) Dedicated Short-Range Communications Service On-Board Units (DSRCS-OBUs). The rules for this service are contained in subpart L of this part. DSRCS-OBUs may communicate with DSRCS Roadside Units (RSUs), which are authorized under part 90 of this chapter. DSRCS, RSU, and OBU are defined in §90.7 of this chapter.

[61 FR 28769, June 6, 1996, as amended at 61 FR 46566, Sept. 4, 1996; 64 FR 69929, Dec. 15, 1999; 65 FR 44008, July 17, 2000; 65 FR 53190, Sept. 1, 2000; 65 FR 60877, Oct. 13, 2000; 67 FR 63289, Oct. 11, 2002; 68 FR 9901, Mar. 3, 2003; 69 FR 46445, Aug. 3, 2004; 74 FR 22705, May 14, 2009]

§95.402 (CB Rule 2) How do I use these rules?

(a) You must comply with these rules (See CB Rule 21 §95.421, for the penalties for violations) when you operate a station in the CB Service from:

(1) Within or over the territorial limits of places where radio services are regulated by the FCC (see CB Rule 5, §95.405);

(2) Aboard any vessel or aircraft registered in the United States; or

(3) Aboard any unregistered vessel or aircraft owned or operated by a United States citizen or company.

(b) Your CB station must comply with technical rules found in subpart E of part 95.

(c) Where the rules use the word "you", "you" means a person operating a CB station.

(d) Where the rules use the word "person," the rules are concerned with an individual, a corporation, a partnership, an association, a joint stock company, a trust, a state, territorial or local government unit, or other legal entity.

(e) Where the rules use the term "FCC", that means the Federal Communications Commission.

(f) Where the rules use the term "CB station", that means a radio station transmitting in the CB Radio Service.

§95.403 (CB Rule 3) Am I eligible to operate a CB station?

You are authorized to operate a CB station unless:

(a) You are a foreign government, a representative of a foreign government, or a federal government agency; or

(b) The FCC has issued a cease and desist order to you, and the order is still in effect.

§95.404 (CB Rule 4) Do I need a license?

You do not need an individual license to operate a CB station. You are authorized by this rule to operate your CB station in accordance with the rules in this subpart.

§95.405 (CB Rule 5) Where may I operate my CB station?

You are authorized to operate your CB station from:

(a) Within or over any area of the world where radio services are regulated by the FCC. Those areas are within the territorial limits of:

Personal Radio Service

(1) The fifty United States.

(2) The District of Columbia.

Caribbean Insular areas

(3) Commonwealth of Puerto Rico.

(4) Navassa Island.

(5) United States Virgin Islands (50 islets and cays).

Pacific Insular areas

(6) American Samoa (seven islands).

(7) Baker Island.

(8) Commonwealth of Northern Mariana Islands.

(9) Guam Island.

(10) Howland Island.

(11) Jarvis Island.

(12) Johnston Island (Islets East, Johnston, North and Sand).

(13) Kingman Reef.

(14) Midway Island (Islets Eastern and Sand).

(15) Palmyra Island (more than 50 islets).

(16) Wake Island (Islets Peale, Wake and Wilkes).

(b) Any other area of the world, except within the territorial limits of areas where radio services are regulated by—

(1) An agency of the United States other than the FCC. (You are subject to its rules.)

(2) Any foreign government. (You are subject to its rules.)

(c) An aircraft or ship, with the permission of the captain, within or over any area of the world where radio services are regulated by the FCC or upon or over international waters. You must operate your CB station according to any applicable treaty to which the United States is a party.

(d) Anyone intending to operate a CB station on the islands of Puerto Rico, Desecheo, Mona, Vieques, and Culebra in a manner that could pose an interference threat to the Arecibo Observatory shall notify the Interference Office, Arecibo Observatory, HC3 Box 53995, Arecibo, Puerto Rico 00612, in writing or electronically, of the location of the unit. Operators may wish to consult interference guidelines, which will be provided by Cornell University. Operators who choose to transmit information electronically should e-mail to: *prcz@naic.edu.*

(1) The notification to the Interference Office, Arecibo Observatory shall be made 45 days prior to commencing operation of the unit. The notification shall state the geographical coordinates of the unit.

(2) After receipt of such notifications, the Commission will allow the Arecibo Observatory a period of 20 days for comments or objections. The operator will be required to make reasonable efforts in order to resolve or mitigate any potential interference problem with the Arecibo Observatory. If the Commission determines that an operator has satisfied its responsibility to make reasonable efforts to protect the Observatory from interference, the unit may be allowed to operate.

[48 FR 24894, June 3, 1983, as amended at 62 FR 55535, Oct. 27, 1997; 70 FR 31374, June 1, 2005]

§95.406 (CB Rule 6) Are there any special restrictions on the location of my CB station?

(a) If your CB station is located on premises controlled by the Department of Defense you may be required to comply with additional regulations imposed by the commanding officer of the installation.

(b) If your C/B station will be constructed on an environmentally sensitive site, or will be operated in such a manner as to raise environmental problems, under §1.1307 of this chapter, you must provide an environmental assessment, as set forth in §1.1311 of this chapter, and undergo the environmental review, §1.1312 of this chapter, before commencement of construction.

[48 FR 24894, June 3, 1983, as amended at 55 FR 20398, May 16, 1990]

How To Operate a CB Station

§95.407 (CB Rule 7) On what channels may I operate?

(a) Your CB station may transmit only on the following channels (frequencies):

Channel	Frequency (Megahertz—MHz)
1	26.965
2	26.975
3	26.985
4	27.005
5	27.015
6	27.025
7	27.035
8	27.055
9	[1]27.065
10	27.075
11	27.085
12	27.105
13	27.115
14	27.125
15	27.135
16	27.155
17	27.165
18	27.175
19	27.185
20	27.205

21	27.215
22	27.225
23	27.255
24	27.235
25	27.245
26	27.265
27	27.275
28	27.285
29	27.295
30	27.305
31	27.315
32	27.325
33	27.335
34	27.345
35	27.355
36	27.365
37	27.375
38	27.385
39	27.395
40	27.405

[1]See paragraph (b) of this section.

(b) Channel 9 may be used only for emergency communications or for traveler assistance.

(c) You must, at all times and on all channels, give priority to emergency communication messages concerning the immediate safety of life or the immediate protection of property.

(d) You may use any channel for emergency communications or for traveler assistance.

(e) You must share each channel with other users.

(f) The FCC will not assign any channel for the private or exclusive use of any particular CB station or group of stations.

(g) The FCC will not assign any channel for the private of exclusive use of CB stations transmitting single sideband or AM.

§95.408 (CB Rule 8) How high may I put my antenna?

(a) *Antenna* means the radiating system (for transmitting, receiving or both) and the structure holding it up (tower, pole or mast). It also means everything else attached to the radiating system and the structure.

(b) If your antenna is mounted on a hand-held portable unit, none of the following limitations apply.

(c) If your antenna is installed at a fixed location, it (whether receiving, transmitting or both) must comply with either one of the following:

(1) The highest point must not be more than 6.10 meters (20 feet) higher than the highest point of the building or tree on which it is mounted; or

(2) The highest point must not be more than 18.3 meters (60 feet) above the ground.

(d) If your CB station is located near an airport, and if you antenna structure is more than 6.1 meters (20 feet) high, you may have to obey additional restrictions. The highest point of your antenna must not exceed one meter above the airport elevation for every hundred meters of distance from the nearest point of the nearest airport runway. Differences in ground elevation between your antenna and the airport runway may complicate this formula. If your CB station is near an airport, you may contact the nearest FCC field office for a worksheet to help you figure the maximum allowable height of your antenna. Consult part 17 of the FCC's Rules for more information.

WARNING: Installation and removal of CB station antennas near power lines is dangerous. For your safety, follow the installation directions included with your antenna.

[48 FR 24894, June 3, 1983, as amended at 48 FR 41416, Sept. 15, 1983]

§95.409 (CB Rule 9) What equipment may I use at my CB station?

(a) You must use an FCC certificated CB transmitter at your CB station. You can identify an FCC certificated transmitter by the certification label placed on it by the manufacturer. You may examine a list of certificated equipment at any FCC Field Office or at FCC Headquarters. Use of a transmitter which is not FCC certificated voids your authority to operate the station.

(b) You must not make, or have made, any internal modification to a certificated CB transmitter. (See CB Rule 25, §95.425). Any internal modification to a certificated CB transmitter cancels the certification, and use of such a transmitter voids your authority to operate the station.

[48 FR 24894, June 3, 1983, as amended at 63 FR 36610, July 7, 1998]

§95.410 (CB Rule 10) How much power may I use?

(a) Your CB station transmitter power output must not exceed the following values under any conditions:

AM (A3)—4 watts (carrier power) SSB—12 watts (peak envelope power)

(b) If you need more information about the power rule, see the technical rules in subpart E of part 95.

(c) Use of a transmitter which has carrier or peak envelope power in excess of that authorized voids your authority to operate the station.

§95.411 (CB Rule 11) May I use power amplifiers?

(a) You may not attach the following items (power amplifiers) to your certificated CB transmitter in any way:

(1) External radio frequency (RF) power amplifiers (sometimes called linear or linear amplifiers); or

(2) Any other devices which, when used with a radio transmitter as a signal source, are capable of amplifying the signal.

(b) There are no exceptions to this rule and use of a power amplifier voids your authority to operate the station.

(c) The FCC will presume you have used a linear or other external RF power amplifier if—

(1) It is in your possession or on your premises; and

(2) There is other evidence that you have operated your CB station with more power than allowed by CB Rule 10, §95.410.

(d) Paragraph (c) of this section does not apply if you hold a license in another radio service which allows you to operate an external RF power amplifier.

[48 FR 24894, June 3, 1983, as amended at 63 FR 36610, July 7, 1998]

§95.412 (CB Rule 12) What communications may be transmitted?

(a) You may use your CB station to transmit two-way plain language communications. Two-way plain language communications are communications without codes or coded messages. Operating signals such as "ten codes" are not considered codes or coded messages. You may transmit two-way plain language communications only to other CB stations, to units of your own CB station or to authorized government stations on CB frequencies about—

(1) Your personal or business activities or those of members of your immediate family living in your household;

(2) Emergencies (see CB Rule 18, §95.418);

(3) Traveler assistance (see CB Rule 18, §95.418); or

(4) Civil defense activities in connection with official tests or drills conducted by, or actual emergencies announced by, the civil defense agency with authority over the area in which your station is located.

(b) You may use your CB station to transmit a tone signal only when the signal is used to make contact or to continue communications. (Examples of circuits using these signals are tone operated squelch and selective calling circuits.) If the signal is an audible tone, it must last no longer than 15 seconds at one time. If the signal is a subaudible tone, it may be transmitted continuously only as long as you are talking.

(c) You may use your CB station to transmit one-way communications (messages which are not intended to establish communications between two or more particular CB stations) only for emergency communications, traveler assistance, brief tests (radio checks) or voice paging.

§95.413 (CB Rule 13) What communications are prohibited?

(a) You must not use a CB station—

(1) In connection with any activity which is against federal, state or local law;

(2) To transmit obscene, indecent or profane words, language or meaning;

(3) To interfere intentionally with the communications of another CB station;

(4) To transmit one-way communications, except for emergency communications, traveler assistance, brief tests (radio checks), or voice paging;

(5) To advertise or solicit the sale of any goods or services;

(6) To transmit music, whistling, sound effects or any material to amuse or entertain;

(7) To transmit any sound effect solely to attract attention;

(8) To transmit the word "MAYDAY" or any other international distress signal, except when your station is located in a ship, aircraft or other vehicle which is threatened by grave and imminent danger and your are requesting immediate assistance;

(9) To communicate with, or attempt to communicate with, any CB station more than 250 kilometers (155.3 miles) away;

(10) To advertise a political candidate or political campaign; (you may use your CB radio for the business or organizational aspects of a campaign, if you follow all other applicable rules);

(11) To communicate with stations in other countries, except General Radio Service stations in Canada; or

(12) To transmit a false or deceptive communication.

(b) You must not use a CB station to transmit communications for live or delayed rebroadcast on a radio or television broadcast station. You may use your CB station to gather news items or to prepare programs.

§95.414 (CB Rule 14) May I be paid to use my CB station?

(a) You may not accept direct or indirect payment for transmitting with a CB station.

(b) You may use a CB station to help you provide a service, and be paid for that service, as long as you are paid only for the service and not for the actual use of the CB station.

§95.415 (CB Rule 15) Who is responsible for communications I make?

You are responsible for all communications which are made by you from a CB station.

§95.416 (CB Rule 16) Do I have to limit the length of my communications?

(a) You must limit your CB communications to the minimum practical time.

(b) If you are communicating with another CB station or stations, you, and the stations communicating with you, must limit each of your conversations to no more than five continuous minutes.

(c) At the end of your conversation, you, and the stations communicating with you, must not transmit again for at least one minute.

§95.417 (CB Rule 17) Do I identify my CB communications?

(a) You need not identify your CB communications.

(b) [You are encouraged to identify your CB communications by any of the following means:

(1) Previously assigned CB call sign;

(2) K prefix followed by operator initials and residence zip code;

(3) Name; or

(4) Organizational description including name and any applicable operator unit number.]

(c) [You are encouraged to use your "handle" only in conjunction with the methods of identification listed in paragraph (b) of this section.]

§95.418 (CB Rule 18) How do I use my CB station in an emergency or to assist a traveler?

(a) You must at all times and on all channels, give priority to emergency communications.

(b) When you are directly participating in emergency communications, you do not have to comply with the rule about length of transmissions (CB Rule 16, §95.416). You must obey all other rules.

(c) You may use your CB station for communications necessary to assist a traveler to reach a destination or to receive necessary services. When you are using your CB station to assist a traveler, you do not have to obey the rule about length of transmissions (CB Rule 16, §95.416). You must obey all other rules.

(d) You may use your CB station to transmit one-way communications concerning highway conditions to assist travelers.

[48 FR 24894, June 3, 1983, as amended at 57 FR 22442, May 28, 1992]

§95.419 (CB Rule 19) May I operate my CB station transmitter by remote control?

(a) You may not operate a CB station transmitter by radio remote control.

(b) You may operate a CB transmitter by wireline remote control if you obtain specific approval in writing from the FCC. To obtain FCC approval, you must show why you need to operate your station by wireline remote control. If you receive FCC approval, you must keep the approval as part of your station records. *See* CB Rule 27, §95.427.

(c) Remote control means operation of a CB transmitter from any place other than the location of the CB transmitter. Direct mechanical control or direct electrical control by wire from some point on the same premises, craft or vehicle as the CB transmitter is not considered remote control.

[48 FR 24894, June 3, 1983, as amended at 57 FR 40343, Sept. 3, 1992; 63 FR 68976, Dec. 14, 1998]

§95.420 (CB Rule 20) May I connect my CB station transmitter to a telephone?

(a) You may connect your CB station transmitter to a telephone if you comply with all of the following:

(1) You or someone else must be present at your CB station and must—

(i) Manually make the connection (the connection must not be made by remote control);

(ii) Supervise the operation of the transmitter during the connection;

(iii) Listen to each communication during the connection; and

(iv) Stop all communications if there are operations in violation of these rules.

(2) Each communication during the telephone connection must comply with all of these rules.

(3) You must obey any restriction that the telephone company places on the connection of a CB transmitter to a telephone.

(b) The CB transmitter you connect to a telephone must not be shared with any other CB station.

(c) If you connect your CB transmitter to a telephone, you must use a phone patch device with has been registered with the FCC.

OTHER THINGS YOU NEED TO KNOW

§95.421 (CB Rule 21) What are the penalties for violating these rules?

(a) If the FCC finds that you have willfully or repeatedly violated the Communications Act or the FCC Rules, you may have to pay as much as $10,000 for each violation, up to a total of $75,000. (See section 503(b) of the Communications Act.)

(b) If the FCC finds that you have violated any section of the Communications Act or the FCC Rules, you may be ordered to stop whatever action caused the violation. (See section 312(b) of the Communications Act.)

(c) If a Federal court finds that you have willfully and knowingly violated any FCC Rule, you may be fined up to $500 for each day you committed the violation. (See section 502 of the Communications Act.)

(d) If a Federal court finds that you have willfully and knowingly violated any provision of the Communications Act, you may be fined up to $10,000 or you may be imprisoned for one year, or both. (See section 501 of the Communications Act.)

[48 FR 24894, June 3, 1983, as amended at 57 FR 40343, Sept. 3, 1992]

§95.422 (CB Rule 22) How do I answer correspondence from the FCC?

(a) If it appears to the FCC that you have violated the Communications Act or these rules, the FCC may send you a discrepancy notice.

(b) Within the time period stated in the notice, you must answer with:

(1) A complete written statement about the apparent discrepancy;

(2) A complete written statement about any action you have taken to correct the apparent violation and to prevent it from happening again; and

(3) The name of the person operating at the time of the apparent violation.

(c) If the FCC sends you a letter asking you questions about your CB radio station or its operation, you must answer each of the questions with a complete written statement within the time period stated in the letter.

(d) You must not shorten your answer by references to other communications or notices.

(e) You must send your answer to the FCC office which sent you the notice.

(f) You must keep a copy of your answer in your station records. (See CB Rule 27, §95.427.)

§95.423 (CB Rule 23) What must I do if the FCC tells me that my CB station is causing interference?

(a) If the FCC tells you that your CB station is causing interference for technical reasons you must follow all instructions in the official FCC notice. (This notice may require you to have technical adjustments made to your equipment.)

(b) You must comply with any restricted hours of CB station operation which may be included in the official notice.

§95.424 (CB Rule 24) How do I have my CB station transmitter serviced?

(a) You may adjust an antenna to your CB transmitter and you may make radio checks. (A radio check means a one way transmission for a short time in order to test the transmitter.)

(b) You are responsible for the proper operation of the station at all times and are expected to provide for observations, servicing and maintenance as often as may be necessary to ensure proper operation. You must have all internal repairs or internal adjustments to your CB transmitter made in accordance with the Technical Regulations (see subpart E). The internal repairs or internal adjustments should be performed by or under the immediate supervision and responsibility of a person certified as technically qualified to perform transmitter maintenance and repair duties in the private land mobile services and fixed services by an organization or committee representative of users in those services.

(c) Except as provided in paragraph (d) of this section, each internal repair and each internal adjustment of a CB transmitter in which signals are transmitted must be made using a nonradiating ("dummy") antenna.

(d) Brief test signals (signals not longer than one minute during any five minute period) using a radiating antenna may be transmitted in order to:

(1) Adjust an antenna to a transmitter;

(2) Detect or measure radiation of energy other than the intended signal; or

(3) Tune a receiver to your CB transmitter.

(Secs. 4(i) and 303(r), Communications Act of 1934, as amended, 47 U.S.C. 154(i) and 303(r), and sec. 553 of the Administrative Procedures Act, 5 U.S.C. 553)

[48 FR 24894, June 3, 1983, as amended at 49 FR 20673, May 16, 1984]

§95.425 (CB Rule 25) May I make any changes to my CB station transmitter?

(a) You must not make or have any one else make any internal modification to your CB transmitter.

(b) Internal modification does not include:

(1) Repair or servicing of a CB station transmitter (see CB Rule 24, §95.424); or

(2) Changing plug-in modules which were certificated as part of your CB transmitter.

(c) You must not operate a CB transmitter which has been modified by anyone in any way, including modification to operate on unauthorized frequencies or with illegal power. (See CB Rules 9 and 11, §§95.409 and 95.411.)

[48 FR 24894, June 3, 1983, as amended at 63 FR 36610, July 7, 1998]

§95.426 (CB Rule 26) Do I have to make my CB station available for inspection?

(a) If an authorized FCC representative requests to inspect your CB station, you must make your CB station and records available for inspection.

(b) A CB station includes all of the radio equipment you use.

§95.427 (CB Rule 27) What are my station records?

Your station records include the following documents, as applicable.

(a) A copy of each response to an FCC violation notice or an FCC letter. (See CB Rule 22, §95.422.)

(b) Each written permission received from the FCC. (See CB Rule 19, §95.419.)

§95.428 (CB Rule 28) How do I contact the FCC?

(a) FCC National Call Center at 1-888-225-5322.

(b) FCC World Wide Web homepage: *http://www.fcc.gov.*

(c) In writing, to FCC, Attention: CB, 1270 Fairfield Road, Gettysburg, PA 17325-7245.

[63 FR 68976, Dec. 14, 1998]

Subpart E—Technical Regulations

SOURCE: 53 FR 36789, Sept. 22, 1988, unless otherwise noted.

GENERAL PROVISIONS

§95.601 Basis and purpose.

This section provides the technical standards to which each transmitter (apparatus that converts electrical energy received from a source into RF (radio frequency) energy capable of being radiated) used or intended to be used in a station authorized in any of the Personal Radio Services must comply. This section also provides requirements for obtaining certification for such transmitters. The Personal Radio Services are the GMRS (General Mobile Radio Service)—subpart A, the Family Radio Service (FRS)—subpart B, the R/C (Radio Control Radio Service)—subpart C, the CB (Citizens Band Radio Service)—subpart D, the Low Power Radio Service (LPRS)—subpart G, the Wireless Medical Telemetry Service (WMTS)—subpart H, the Medical Device Radio communication Service (MedRadio)—subpart I, the Multi-Use Radio Service (MURS)—subpart J, and Dedicated Short-Range Communications Service On-Board Units (DSRCS-OBUs)—subpart L.

[69 FR 46445, Aug. 3, 2004, as amended at 74 FR 22705, May 14, 2009]

§95.603 Certification required.

(a) Each *GMRS transmitter* (a transmitter that operates or is intended to operate at a station authorized in the GMRS) must be certificated.

(b) Each *R/C transmitter* (a transmitter that operates or is intended to operate at a station authorized in the R/C) must be certificated, except one that transmits only in the 26-27 MHz frequency band and is *crystal controlled* (where the transmitted frequency is established by a *crystal* (a quartz piezo-electric element)).

70

(c) Each *CB transmitter* (a transmitter that operates or is intended to operate at a station authorized in the CB) must be certificated. No CB transmitter certificated pursuant to an application filed prior to September 10, 1976, shall be manufactured or marketed.

(d) Each FRS unit (a transmitter that operates or is intended to operate in the FRS) must be certified for use in the FRS in accordance with subpart J of part 2 of this chapter.

(e) Each Low Power Radio Service transmitter (a transmitter that operates or is intended to operate in the LPRS) must be certificated.

(f) Each Medical Device Radio communication Service (MedRadio) transmitter (a transmitter that operates or is intended to operate in the MedRadio service) must be certificated except for such transmitters that are not marketed for use in the United States, but which otherwise comply with the MedRadio Service technical requirements and are operated in the United States by individuals who have traveled to the United States from abroad.

(g) Each Multi-Use Radio Service transmitter (a transmitter that operates or is intended to operate in the MURS) must be certificated in accordance with subpart J of part 2 of this chapter, Provided however, that those radio units certificated as of November 12, 2002 need not be recertificated.

(h) Each Dedicated Short-Range Communications Service On-Board Unit (DSRCS-OBU) that operates or is intended to operate in the DSRCS (5.850-5.925 GHz) must be certified in accordance with subpart L of this part and subpart J of part 2 of this chapter.

[53 FR 36789, Sept. 22, 1988, as amended at 61 FR 28769, June 6, 1996; 61 FR 46567, Sept. 4, 1996; 63 FR 36610, July 7, 1998; 64 FR 69929, Dec. 15, 1999; 65 FR 60877, Oct. 13, 2000; 67 FR 63289, Oct. 11, 2002; 69 FR 46446, Aug. 3, 2004; 74 FR 22705, May 14, 2009]

§95.605 Certification procedures.

Any entity may request certification for its transmitter when the transmitter is used in the GMRS, FRS, R/C, CB, 218-219 MHz Service, LPRS, MURS, or MedRadio Service following the procedures in part 2 of this chapter. Dedicated Short-Range Communications Service On-Board Units (DSRCS-OBUs) must be certified in accordance with subpart L of this part and subpart J of part 2 of this chapter.

[74 FR 22705, May 14, 2009]

§95.607 CB transmitter modification.

Only the holder of the grant of authorization of the particular certificated CB transmitter may make the modifications permitted under the provisions for certification (see part 2 of this chapter.) No grantee shall make any of the following modifications to the transmitter without prior written permission from the *FCC* (Federal Communications Commission):

(a) The addition of any accessory or device not specified in the application for certification and authorized by the FCC in granting the certification;

(b) The addition of any switch, control or external connection;

(c) Any modification to provide for additional transmitting frequencies, increased modulation level, a different form of modulation, or increased *TP* (RF transmitter power expressed in *W* (watts), either *mean power* (TP averaged over at least 30 cycles of the lowest modulating frequency, typically 0.1 seconds at maximum power) or *peak envelope power* (TP averaged during 1 RF cycle at the highest crest of the modulation envelope), as measured at the transmitter output antenna terminals.)

[53 FR 36789, Sept. 22, 1988, as amended at 63 FR 36610, July 7, 1998]

TECHNICAL STANDARDS

§95.621 GMRS transmitter channel frequencies.

(a) The GMRS transmitter *channel frequencies* (reference frequencies from which the carrier frequency, suppressed or otherwise, may not deviate by more than the specified frequency tolerance) are 462.5500, 462.5625, 462.5750, 462.5875, 462.6000, 462.6125, 462.6250, 462.6375, 462.6500, 462.6625, 462.6750, 462.6875, 462.7000, 462.7125, 462.7250, 467.5500, 467.5750, 467.6000, 467.6250, 467.6500, 467.6750, 467.7000, and 467.7250.

NOTE: Certain GMRS transmitter channel frequencies are authorized only for certain station classes and station locations. *See* part 95, subpart A.

(b) Each GMRS transmitter for mobile station, small base station and control station operation must be maintained within a frequency tolerance of 0.0005%. Each GMRS transmitter for base station (except small base), mobile relay station or fixed station operation must be maintained within a frequency tolerance of 0.00025%.

[53 FR 47718, Nov. 25, 1988]

§95.623 R/C transmitter channel frequencies.

(a) The R/C transmitter channel frequencies are:

MHz

26.995	72.75
27.045	72.77
27.095	72.79
27.145	72.81
27.195	72.83
27.255	72.85
72.01	72.87

72.03	72.89
72.05	72.91
72.07	72.93
72.09	72.95
72.11	72.97
72.13	72.99
72.15	75.41
72.17	75.43
72.19	75.45
72.21	75.47
72.23	75.49
72.25	75.51
72.27	75.53
72.29	75.55
72.31	75.57
72.33	75.59
72.35	75.61
72.37	75.63
72.39	75.65
72.41	75.67
72.43	75.69
72.45	75.71
72.47	75.73
72.49	75.75
72.51	75.77
72.53	75.79
72.55	75.81
72.57	75.83
72.59	75.85
72.61	75.87
72.63	75.89
72.65	75.91
72.67	75.93
72.69	75.95

Personal Radio Service

72.71   75.97

72.73   75.99

NOTE: Certain R/C transmitter channel frequencies are authorized to operate only certain kinds of devices (see part 95, subpart C.)

(b) Each R/C transmitter that transmits in the 26-27 MHz frequency band with a mean TP of 2.5 W or less and that is used solely by the operator to turn on and/or off a device at a remote location, other than a device used solely to attract attention, must be maintained within a frequency tolerance of 0.01%. All other R/C transmitters that transmit in the 26-27 MHz frequency band must be maintained within a frequency tolerance of 0.005%. Except as noted in paragraph (c) of this section, R/C transmitters capable of operation in the 72-76 MHz band must be maintained within a frequency tolerance of 0.005%.

(c) All R/C transmitters capable of operation in the 72-76 MHz band that are manufactured in or imported into the United States, on or after March 1, 1992, or are marketed on or after March 1, 1993, must be maintained within a frequency tolerance of 0.002%. R/C transmitters operating in the 72-76 MHz band and marketed before March 1, 1993, may continue to be operated with a frequency tolerance of 0.005% until March 1, 1998.

[53 FR 36789, Sept. 22, 1988; 53 FR 52713, Dec. 29, 1988; 56 FR 15837, Apr. 18, 1991]

§95.625 CB transmitter channel frequencies.

(a) The CB transmitter channel frequencies are:

Channel No.	(MHz)
1	26.965
2	26.975
3	26.985
4	27.005
5	27.015
6	27.025
7	27.035
8	27.055
9	27.065
10	27.075
11	27.085
12	27.105
13	27.115
14	27.125
15	27.135
16	27.155
17	27.165
18	27.175
19	27.185
20	27.205
21	27.215
22	27.225

23	27.255
24	27.235
25	27.245
26	27.265
27	27.275
28	27.285
29	27.295
30	27.305
31	27.315
32	27.325
33	27.335
34	27.345
35	27.355
36	27.365
37	27.375
38	27.385
39	27.395
40	27.405

(b) Each CB transmitter must be maintained within a frequency tolerance of 0.005%.

§95.626 FRS unit channel frequencies.

(a) The FRS unit channel frequencies are:

Channel No.	(MHz)
1	462.5625
2	462.5875
3	462.6125
4	462.6375
5	462.6625
6	462.6875
7	462.7125
8	467.5625
9	467.5875
10	467.6125
11	467.6375
12	467.6625
13	467.6875
14	467.7125

(b) Each FRS unit must be maintained within a frequency tolerance of 0.00025%.

[61 FR 28769, June 6, 1996. Redesignated at 77 FR 4268, Jan. 27, 2012]

§95.627 MedRadio transmitters in the 401-406 MHz band.

The following provisions apply only to MedRadio transmitters operating in the 401-406 MHz band.

(a) *Frequency monitoring.* Except as provided in (b) of this section, all MedRadio programmer/control transmitters operating in the 401-406 MHz band must operate under the control of a monitoring system that incorporates a mechanism for monitoring the channel or channels that the MedRadio system devices intend to occupy. The monitoring system antenna shall be the antenna normally used by the programmer/control transmitter for a communications session. Before the monitoring system of a MedRadio programmer/control transmitter initiates a MedRadio communications session, the following access criteria must be met:

(1) The monitoring system bandwidth measured at its 20 dB down points must be equal to or greater than the emission bandwidth of the intended transmission.

(2) Within 5 seconds prior to initiating a communications session, circuitry associated with a MedRadio programmer/control transmitter must monitor the channel or channels the system devices intend to occupy for a minimum of 10 milliseconds per channel.

(3) Based on use of an isotropic monitoring system antenna, the monitoring threshold power level must not be more than $10 \log B(Hz) -150$ (dBm/Hz) + G(dBi), where B is the emission bandwidth of the MedRadio communications session transmitter having the widest emission and G is the MedRadio programmer/control transmitter monitoring system antenna gain relative to an isotropic antenna. For purposes of showing compliance with the above provision, the above calculated threshold power level must be increased or decreased by an amount equal to the monitoring system antenna gain above or below the gain of an isotropic antenna, respectively.

(4) If no signal in a MedRadio channel above the monitoring threshold power level is detected, the MedRadio programmer/control transmitter may initiate a MedRadio-communications session involving transmissions to and from a medical implant or medical body-worn device on that channel. The MedRadio communications session may continue as long as any silent period between consecutive data transmission bursts

does not exceed 5 seconds. If a channel meeting the criteria in paragraph (a)(3) of this section is unavailable, MedRadio transmitters that are capable of operating on multiple channels may transmit on the alternate channel accessible by the device with the lowest monitored ambient power level. Except as provided in paragraph (b) of this section, MedRadio transmitters that operate on a single channel and thus do not have the capability of operating on alternate channels may not transmit unless no signal on the single channel of operation exceeds the monitoring threshold power level.

(5) When a channel is selected prior to a MedRadio communications session, it is permissible to select an alternate channel for use if communications are interrupted, provided that the alternate channel selected is the next best choice using the above criteria. The alternate channel may be accessed in the event a communications session is interrupted by interference. The following criteria must be met:

(i) Before transmitting on the alternate channel, the channel must be monitored for a period of at least 10 milliseconds.

(ii) The detected power level during this 10 millisecond or greater monitoring period must be no higher than 6dB above the power level detected when the channel was chosen as the alternate channel.

(iii) In the event that this alternate channel provision is not used by the MedRadio system or if the criteria in paragraphs (a)(5)(i) and (ii) are not met, a channel must be selected using the access criteria specified in paragraphs (a)(1) through (a)(4) of this section.

(6) As used in this section, the following definitions apply:

(i) *Emission bandwidth*— Measured as the width of the signal between the points on either side of carrier center frequency that are 20 dB down relative to the maximum level of the modulated carrier. Compliance will be determined using instrumentation employing a peak detector function and a resolution bandwidth approximately equal to 1% of the emission bandwidth of the device under test.

(ii) *MedRadio channel*—Any continuous segment of spectrum in the MedRadio band that is equal to the emission bandwidth of the device with the largest bandwidth that is to participate in a MedRadio communications session.

NOTE TO PARAGRAPH (a)(6)(ii): The rules do not specify a channeling scheme for use by MedRadio systems.

(iii) *MedRadio communications session*—A collection of transmissions, that may or may not be continuous, between MedRadio system devices.

(b) *Exceptions to frequency monitoring criteria.* MedRadio devices or communications sessions that meet any one of the following criteria are not required to use the access criteria set forth in paragraph (a) of this section:

(1) MedRadio communications sessions initiated by a medical implant event.

(2) MedRadio devices operating in either the 401-401.85 MHz or 405-406 MHz bands, provided that the transmit power is not greater than 250 nanowatts EIRP and the duty cycle for such transmissions does not exceed 0.1%, based on the total transmission time during a one-hour interval, and a maximum of 100 transmissions per hour.

(3) MedRadio devices operating in the 401.85-402 MHz band, provided that the transmit power is not greater than 25 microwatts EIRP and the duty cycle for such transmissions does not exceed 0.1%, based on the total transmission time during a one hour interval, and a maximum of 100 transmissions per hour.

(4) MedRadio devices operating with a total emission bandwidth not exceeding 300 kHz centered at 403.65 MHz, provided that the transmit power is not greater than 100 nanowatts EIRP and the duty cycle for such transmissions does not exceed 0.01%, based on the total transmission time during a one-hour interval, and a maximum of 10 transmissions per hour.

(c) *Operating frequency.* MedRadio stations authorized under this part may operate on frequencies in the 401-406 MHz band as follows provided that the out-of-band emissions are attenuated in accordance with §95.635:

(1) MedRadio stations associated with medical implant devices, which incorporate a frequency monitoring system as set forth in paragraph (a) of this section, may operate on any of the frequencies in the 401-406 MHz band.

(2) MedRadio stations associated with medical implant devices, which do not incorporate a frequency monitoring system as set forth in paragraph (a) of this section, may operate on any frequency in 401-402 MHz or 405-406 MHz bands, or at 403.65 MHz in the 402-405 MHz band.

(3) MedRadio stations associated with medical body-worn devices, regardless of whether a frequency monitoring system as set forth in paragraph (a) of this section is employed, may operate on any of the frequencies in the 401-402 MHz or 405-406 MHz bands.

(4) MedRadio stations that are used externally to evaluate the efficacy of a more permanent medical implant device, regardless of whether a frequency monitoring system as set forth in paragraph (a) of this section is employed, may operate on any of the frequencies in the 402-405 MHz band, provided that:

(i) Such external body-worn operation is limited solely to evaluating with a patient the efficacy of a fully implanted permanent medical device that is intended to replace the temporary body-worn device;

(ii) RF transmissions from the external device must cease following the patient evaluation period, which may not exceed 30 days, except where a health care practitioner determines that additional time is necessary due to unforeseen circumstances;

(iii) The maximum output power of the temporary body-worn device shall not exceed 200 nW EIRP; and

(iv) The temporary body-worn device must comply fully with all other MedRadio rules applicable to medical implant device operation in the 402-405 MHz band.

(d) *Authorized bandwidth.* The authorized bandwidth of the emission from a MedRadio station operating between 402-405 MHz shall not exceed 300 kHz, and no communications session involving MedRadio stations shall use more than a total of 300 kHz of bandwidth during such a session. The authorized bandwidth of the emission from a MedRadio station operating between 401-401.85 MHz or 405-406 MHz shall not exceed 100 kHz, and no communications session involving MedRadio stations shall use more than a total of 100 kHz of bandwidth during such a session. The authorized bandwidth of the emission from a MedRadio station operating between 401.85-402 MHz shall not exceed 150 kHz, and no communications session involving MedRadio stations shall use more than a total of 150 kHz of bandwidth during such a session.

NOTE TO PARAGRAPH (d): This provision does not preclude full duplex or half duplex communications provided that the total amount of bandwidth utilized by all of the MedRadio channels employed in such a MedRadio communications session does not exceed 300 kHz in the 402-405 MHz band, or 100 kHz in the 401-402 MHz and 405-406 MHz bands.

(e) *Frequency stability.* Each transmitter in the MedRadio service must maintain a frequency stability of ±100 ppm of the operating frequency over the range:

(1) 25 °C to 45 °C in the case of medical implant transmitters; and

(2) 0 °C to 55 °C in the case of MedRadio programmer/control transmitters and MedRadio body-worn transmitters.

(f) *Shared access.* The provisions of this section shall not be used to extend the range of spectrum occupied over space or time for the purpose of denying fair access to spectrum for other MedRadio systems.

(g) *Measurement procedures.* (1) MedRadio transmitters shall be tested for frequency stability, radiated emissions and EIRP limit compliance in accordance with paragraphs (g)(2) and (g)(3) of this section.

(3) Radiated emissions and EIRP measurements may be determined by measuring the radiated field from the equipment under test at 3 meters and calculating the EIRP. The equivalent radiated field strength at 3 meters for 25 microwatts, 250 nanowatts, and 100 nanowatts EIRP is 18.2, 1.8, or 1.2 mV/meter, respectively, when measured on an open area test site; or 9.1, 0.9, or 0.6 mV/meter, respectively, when measured on a test site equivalent to free space such as a fully anechoic test chamber. Compliance with the maximum transmitter power requirements set forth in §95.639(f) shall be based on measurements using a peak detector function and measured over an interval of time when transmission is continuous and at its maximum power level. In lieu of using a peak detector function, measurement procedures that have been found to be acceptable to the Commission in accordance with §2.947 of this chapter may be used to demonstrate compliance.

(2) Frequency stability testing shall be performed over the temperature range set forth in (e) of this section.

(3) Radiated emissions and EIRP measurements may be determined by measuring the radiated field from the equipment under test at 3 meters and calculating the EIRP. The equivalent radiated field strength at 3 meters for 25 microwatts, 250 nanowatts, and 100 nanowatts EIRP is 18.2, 1.8, or 1.2 mV/meter, respectively, when measured on an open area test site; or 9.1, 0.9, or 0.6 mV/meter, respectively, when measured on a test site equivalent to free space such as a fully anechoic test chamber. Compliance with the maximum transmitter power requirements set forth in §95.639(f) shall be based on measurements using a peak detector function and measured over an interval of time when transmission is continuous and at its maximum power level. In lieu of using a peak detector function, measurement procedures that have been found to be acceptable to the Commission in accordance with §2.947 of this chapter may be used to demonstrate compliance.

84

(i) For a transmitter intended to be implanted in a human body, radiated emissions and EIRP measurements for transmissions by stations authorized under this section may be made in accordance with a Commission-approved human body simulator and test technique. A formula for a suitable tissue substitute material is defined in OET Bulletin 65 Supplement C (01-01).

[74 FR 22705, May 14, 2009, as amended at 75 FR 52477, Aug. 26, 2010. Redesignated and amended at 77 FR 4268, Jan. 27, 2012]

§95.628 MedRadio transmitters in the 413-419 MHz, 426-432 MHz, 438-444 MHz, and 451-457 MHz and 2360-2400 MHz bands.

The following provisions apply to MedRadio transmitters operating in the 413-419 MHz, 426-432 MHz, 438-444 MHz, and 451-457 MHz bands as part of a Medical Micropower Network (MMN) and in the 2360-2400 MHz band as part of a Medical Body Area Network (MBAN).

(a) *Operating frequencies.* A MedRadio station authorized under this part must have out-of-band emissions that are attenuated in accordance with §95.635.

(1) Only MedRadio stations that are part of an MMN may operate in the 413-419 MHz, 426-432 MHz, 438-444 MHz, and 451-457 MHz frequency bands. Each MedRadio station that is part of an MMN must be capable of operating in each of the following frequency bands: 413-419 MHz, 426-432 MHz, 438-444 MHz, and 451-457 MHz. All MedRadio stations that are part of a single MMN must operate in the same frequency band.

(2) Only MedRadio stations that are part of an MBAN may operate in the 2360-2400 MHz frequency band.

(b) *Requirements for a Medical Micropower Network.* (1) *Frequency monitoring.* MedRadio programmer/control transmitters must incorporate a mechanism for monitoring the authorized bandwidth of the frequency band that the MedRadio transmitters intend to occupy. The monitoring system antenna shall be the antenna used by the programmer/control transmitter for a communications session.

(i) The MedRadio programmer/control transmitter shall be capable of monitoring any occupied frequency band at least once every second and monitoring alternate frequency bands within two seconds prior to executing a change to an alternate frequency band.

(ii) The MedRadio programmer/control transmitter shall move to another frequency band within one second of detecting a persistent (*i.e.*, lasting more than 50 milliseconds in duration) signal level greater than −60 dBm as received by a 0 dBi gain antenna in any 12.5 kHz bandwidth within the authorized bandwidth.

(iii) The MedRadio programmer/control transmitter shall be capable of monitoring the authorized bandwidth of the occupied frequency band to determine whether either direction of the communications link is becoming degraded to the extent that communications is likely to be lost for more than 45 milliseconds. Upon making such a determination the MedRadio programmer/control transmitter shall move to another frequency band.

(2) *MedRadio transmitters.* MedRadio transmitters shall incorporate a programmable means to implement a system shutdown process in the event of communication failure, on command from the MedRadio programmer/control transmitter, or when no frequency band is available. The shutdown process shall commence within 45 milliseconds after loss of the communication link or receipt of the shutdown command from the MedRadio programmer/control transmitter.

(3) *MedRadio programmer/control transmitters.* MedRadio programmer/control transmitters shall have the ability to operate in the presence of other primary and secondary users in the 413-419 MHz, 426-432 MHz, 438-444 MHz, and 451-457 MHz bands.

86

(4) *Authorized bandwidth.* The 20 dB authorized bandwidth of the emission from a MedRadio station operating in the 413-419 MHz, 426-432 MHz, 438-444 MHz, and 451-457 MHz bands shall not exceed 6 MHz.

(c) *Requirements for Medical Body Area Networks.* A MedRadio programmer/control transmitter shall not commence operating and shall automatically cease operating in the 2360-2390 MHz band if it does not receive, in accordance with the protocols specified by the manufacturer, a control message permitting such operation Additionally, a MedRadio programmer/control transmitter operating in the 2360-2390 MHz band shall comply with a control message that notifies the device to limit its transmissions to segments of the 2360-2390 MHz band or to cease operation in the band.

(d) *Frequency stability.* Each transmitter in the MedRadio service must maintain a frequency stability of ±100 ppm of the operating frequency over the range:

(1) 25 °C to 45 °C in the case of medical implant transmitters; and

(2) 0 °C to 55 °C in the case of MedRadio programmer/control transmitters and Medical body-worn transmitters.

(e) *Shared access.* The provisions of this section shall not be used to extend the range of spectrum occupied over space or time for the purpose of denying fair access to spectrum for other MedRadio systems.

(f) *Measurement procedures.* (1) MedRadio transmitters shall be tested for frequency stability, radiated emissions and EIRP limit compliance in accordance with paragraphs (f)(2) and (3) of this section.

(2) Frequency stability testing shall be performed over the temperature range set forth in (d) of this section.

(3) Radiated emissions and EIRP limit measurements may be determined by measuring the radiated field from the equipment under test at 3 meters and calculating the EIRP. The equivalent radiated field strength at 3 meters for 1 milliwatt, 25 microwatts, 250 nanowatts, and 100 nanowatts EIRP is 115.1, 18.2, 1.8, or 1.2 mV/meter, respectively, when measured on an open area test site; or 57.55, 9.1, 0.9, or 0.6 mV/meter, respectively, when measured on a test site equivalent to free space such as a fully anechoic test chamber. Compliance with the maximum transmitter power requirements set forth in §95.639(f) shall be based on measurements using a peak detector function and measured over an interval of time when transmission is continuous and at its maximum power level. In lieu of using a peak detector function, measurement procedures that have been found to be acceptable to the Commission in accordance with §2.947 of this chapter may be used to demonstrate compliance. For a transmitter intended to be implanted in a human body, radiated emissions and EIRP measurements for transmissions by stations authorized under this section may be made in accordance with a Commission-approved human body simulator and test technique. A formula for a suitable tissue substitute material is defined in OET Bulletin 65 Supplement C (01-01).

[77 FR 55732, Sept. 11, 2012]

§95.629 LPRS transmitter frequencies.

(a) LPRS transmitters may operate on any frequency listed in paragraphs (b), (c), and (d) of this section. Channels 19, 20, 50, and 151-160 are available exclusively for law enforcement tracking purposes. AMTS transmissions are limited to the 216.750-217.000 MHz band for low power point-to-point network control communications by AMTS coast stations. Other AMTS transmissions in the 216-217 MHz band are prohibited.

(b) *Standard band channels.* (1) The following table indicates standard band frequencies. The channel bandwidth is 25 kHz.

Channel No.	Center frequency (MHz)
1	216.0125
2	216.0375
3	216.0625
4	216.0875
5	216.1125
6	216.1375
7	216.1625
8	216.1875
9	216.2125
10	216.2375
11	216.2625
12	216.2875
13	216.3125
14	216.3375
15	216.3625

16	216.3875
17	216.4125
18	216.4375
19	216.4625
20	216.4875
21	216.5125
22	216.5375
23	216.5625
24	216.5875
25	216.6125
26	216.6375
27	216.6625
28	216.6875
29	216.7125
30	216.7375
31	216.7625
32	216.7875
33	216.8125
34	216.8375
35	216.8625
36	216.8875
37	216.9125
38	216.9375
39	216.9625
40	216.9875

Personal Radio Service

(2) LPRS transmitters operating on standard band channels must be maintained within a frequency stability of 50 parts per million.

(c) *Extra band channels.* (1) The following table indicates extra band frequencies. The channel bandwidth is 50 kHz.

Channel No.	Center frequency (MHz)
41	216.025
42	216.075
43	216.125
44	216.175
45	216.225
46	216.275
47	216.325
48	216.375
49	216.425
50	216.475
51	216.525
52	216.575
53	216.625
54	216.675
55	216.725
56	216.775
57	216.825
58	216.875
59	216.925
60	216.975

(2) LPRS transmitters operating on extra band channels must be maintained within a frequency stability of 50 parts per million.

(d) *Narrowband channels.* (1) The following table indicates narrowband frequencies. The channel bandwidth is 5 kHz and the authorized bandwidth is 4 kHz.

Channel No.	Center frequency (MHz)
61	216.0025
62	216.0075
63	216.0125
64	216.0175
65	216.0225
66	216.0275
67	216.0325
68	216.0375
69	216.0425
70	216.0475
71	216.0525
72	216.0575
73	216.0625
74	216.0675
75	216.0725
76	216.0775
77	216.0825
78	216.0875
79	216.0925
80	216.0975

81	216.1025
82	216.1075
83	216.1125
84	216.1175
85	216.1225
86	216.1275
87	216.1325
88	216.1375
89	216.1425
90	216.1475
91	216.1525
92	216.1575
93	216.1625
94	216.1675
95	216.1725
96	216.1775
97	216.1825
98	216.1875
99	216.1925
100	216.1975
101	216.2025
102	216.2075
103	216.2125
104	216.2175
105	216.2225

106	216.2275
107	216.2325
108	216.2375
109	216.2425
110	216.2475
111	216.2525
112	216.2575
113	216.2625
114	216.2675
115	216.2725
116	216.2775
117	216.2825
118	216.2875
119	216.2925
120	216.2975
121	216.3025
122	216.3075
123	216.3125
124	216.3175
125	216.3225
126	216.3275
127	216.3325
128	216.3375
129	216.3425
130	216.3475
131	216.3525

132	216.3575
133	216.3625
134	216.3675
135	216.3725
136	216.3775
137	216.3825
138	216.3875
139	216.3925
140	216.3975
141	216.4025
142	216.4075
143	216.4125
144	216.4175
145	216.4225
146	216.4275
147	216.4325
148	216.4375
149	216.4425
150	216.4475
151	216.4525
152	216.4575
153	216.4625
154	216.4675
155	216.4725
156	216.4775

157	216.4825
158	216.4875
159	216.4925
160	216.4975
161	216.5025
162	216.5075
163	216.5125
164	216.5175
165	216.5225
166	216.5275
167	216.5325
168	216.5375
169	216.5425
170	216.5475
171	216.5525
172	216.5575
173	216.5625
174	216.5675
175	216.5725
176	216.5775
177	216.5825
178	216.5875
179	216.5925
180	216.5975
181	216.6025
182	216.6075

183	216.6125
184	216.6175
185	216.6225
186	216.6275
187	216.6325
188	216.6375
189	216.6425
190	216.6475
191	216.6525
192	216.6575
193	216.6625
194	216.6675
195	216.6725
196	216.6775
197	216.6825
198	216.6875
199	216.6925
200	216.6975
201	216.7025
202	216.7075
203	216.7125
204	216.7175
205	216.7225
206	216.7275
207	216.7325

208	216.7375
209	216.7425
210	216.7475
211	216.7525
212	216.7575
213	216.7625
214	216.7675
215	216.7725
216	216.7775
217	216.7825
218	216.7875
219	216.7925
220	216.7975
221	216.8025
222	216.8075
223	216.8125
224	216.8175
225	216.8225
226	216.8275
227	216.8325
228	216.8375
229	216.8425
230	216.8475
231	216.8525
232	216.8575
233	216.8625

234	216.8675
235	216.8725
236	216.8775
237	216.8825
238	216.8875
239	216.8925
240	216.8975
241	216.9025
242	216.9075
243	216.9125
244	216.9175
245	216.9225
246	216.9275
247	216.9325
248	216.9375
249	216.9425
250	216.9475
251	216.9525
252	216.9575
253	216.9625
254	216.9675
255	216.9725
256	216.9775
257	216.9825
258	216.9875

259	216.9925
260	216.9975

(2) LPRS transmitters operating on narrowband channels must be maintained within a frequency stability of 1.5 parts per million.

[61 FR 46567, Sept. 4, 1996]

§95.630 WMTS Transmitter frequencies.

WMTS transmitters may operate in the frequency bands specified as follows:

608-614 MHz

1395-1400 MHz

1427-1429.5 MHz except at the locations listed in §90.259(b)(4) where WMTS may operate in the 1429-1431.5 MHz band.

[69 FR 39868, July 1, 2004]

§95.631 Emission types.

(a) A GMRS transmitter must transmit only emission types A1D, F1D, G1D, H1D, J1D, R1D, A3E, F3E, G3E, H3E, J3E or R3E. A non-voice emission is limited to selective calling or tone-operated squelch tones to establish or continue voice communications. See §95.181 (g) and (h).

(b) An R/C transmitter may transmit any appropriate non-voice emission which meets the emission limitations of §95.633.

(c) A CB transmitter may transmit only emission types A1D, H1D, J1D, R1D, A3E, H3E, J3E, R3E. A non-voice emission is limited to selective calling or tone-operated squelch tones to establish or continue voice communications. See §95.412 (b) and (c).

100

(d) An FRS unit may transmit only emission type F3E or F2D. A non-voice emission is limited to selective calling or tone-operated squelch tones to establish or continue voice communications, digital data transmission of location information or text messaging.

(e) No GMRS or CB transmitter shall employ a digital modulation or emission.

(f) No GMRS, CB or R/C transmitter shall transmit non-voice data.

(g) An LPRS station may transmit any emission type appropriate for communications in this service. Two-way voice communications, however, are prohibited.

(h) A MedRadio station may transmit any emission type appropriate for communications in this service. Voice communications, however, are prohibited.

(i) A WMTS station may transmit any emission type appropriate for communications in this service, except for video and voice. Waveforms such as electrocardiograms (ECGs) are not considered video.

(j) A MURS transmitter must transmit only emission types A1D, A2B, A2D, A3E, F2B, F1D, F2D, F3E, G3E. Emission types A3E, F3E and G3E include selective calling or tone-operated squelch tones to establish or continue voice communications. MURS transmitters are prohibited from transmitting in the continuous carrier mode.

(k) DSRCS-OBUs are governed under subpart L of this part.

[53 FR 36789, Sept. 22, 1988. Redesignated and amended at 61 FR 28769, June 6, 1996, and further redesignated and amended at 61 FR 46567, 46568, Sept. 4, 1996; 64 FR 69930, Dec. 15, 1999; 65 FR 44008, July 17, 2000; 65 FR 53190, Sept. 1, 2000; 65 FR 60877, Oct. 13, 2000; 67 FR 63289, Oct. 11, 2002; 68 FR 9901, Mar. 3, 2003; 69 FR 46446, Aug. 3, 2004; 74 FR 22706, May 14, 2009]

§95.632 MURS transmitter frequencies.

(a) The MURS transmitter channel frequencies are 151.820 MHz, 151.880 MHz, 151.940 MHz, 154.570 MHz, 154.600 MHz.

(b) The authorized bandwidth is 11.25 kHz on frequencies 151.820 MHz, 151.880 MHz and 151.940 MHz. The authorized bandwidth is 20.0 kHz on frequencies 154.570 and 154.600 MHz.

(c) MURS transmitters must maintain a frequency stability of 5.0 ppm, or 2.0 ppm if designed to operate with a 6.25 kHz bandwidth.

[65 FR 60877, Oct. 13, 2000, as amended at 67 FR 63289, Oct. 11, 2002]

§95.633 Emission bandwidth.

(a) The *authorized bandwidth* (maximum permissible bandwidth of a transmission) for emission type H1D, J1D, R1D, H3E, J3E or R3E is 4 kHz. The authorized bandwidth for emission type A1D or A3E is 8 kHz. The authorized bandwidth for emission type F1D, G1D, F3E or G3E is 20 kHz.

(b) The authorized bandwidth for any emission type transmitted by an R/C transmitter is 8 kHz.

(c) The authorized bandwidth for emission type F3E or F2D transmitted by a FRS unit is 12.5 kHz.

(d) For transmitters in the LPRS:

(1) The authorized bandwidth for narrowband frequencies is 4 kHz and the channel bandwidth is 5 kHz

(2) The channel bandwidth for standard band frequencies is 25 kHz.

(3) The channel bandwidth for extra band frequencies is 50 kHz.

102

(4) AMTS stations may use the 216.750-217.000 MHz band as a single 250 kHz channel so long as the signal is attenuated as specified in §95.635(c).

(e) For transmitters in the MedRadio Service:

(1) For stations operating in 402-405 MHz, the maximum authorized emission bandwidth is 300 kHz. For stations operating in 401-401.85 MHz or 405-406 MHz, the maximum authorized emission bandwidth is 100 kHz. For stations operating in 401.85-402 MHz, the maximum authorized emission bandwidth is 150 kHz. For stations operating in 413-419 MHz, 426-432 MHz, 438-444 MHz, or 451-457 MHz, the maximum authorized emission bandwidth is 6 megahertz. For stations operating in 2360-2400 MHz, the maximum authorized emission bandwidth is 5 megahertz.

(2) Lesser emission bandwidths may be employed, provided that the unwanted emissions are attenuated as provided in §95.635. See §§95.627(g), §95.628(h), and 95.639(f) regarding maximum transmitter power and measurement procedures.

(3) Emission bandwidth will be determined by measuring the width of the signal between points, one below the carrier center frequency and one above the carrier center frequency, that are 20 dB down relative to the maximum level of the modulated carrier. Compliance with the emission bandwidth limit is based on the use of measurement instrumentation employing a peak detector function with an instrument resolution bandwidth approximately equal to 1.0 percent of the emission bandwidth of the device under measurement.

(f) The authorized bandwidth for any emission type transmitted by a MURS transmitter is specified as follows:

(1) Emissions on frequencies 151.820 MHz, 151.880 MHz, and 151.940 MHz are limited to 11.25 kHz.

(2) Emissions on frequencies 154.570 and 154.600 MHz are limited to 20.0 kHz.

(3) Provided, however, that all A3E emissions are limited to 8 kHz.

(g) DSRCS-OBUs are governed under subpart L of this part.

[53 FR 36789, Sept. 22, 1988. Redesignated and amended at 61 FR 28769, June 6, 1996, and further redesignated and amended at 61 FR 46567, 46568, Sept. 4, 1996; 64 FR 69930, Dec. 15, 1999; 65 FR 60878, Oct. 13, 2000; 67 FR 63289, Oct. 11, 2002; 68 FR 9902, Mar. 3, 2003; 69 FR 46446, Aug. 3, 2004; 74 FR 22707, May 14, 2009; 77 FR 4268, Jan. 27, 2012; 77 FR 55733, Sept. 11, 2012]

§95.635 Unwanted radiation.

(a) In addition to the procedures in part 2, the following requirements apply to each transmitter both with and without the connection of all attachments acceptable for use with the transmitter, such as an external speaker, microphone, power cord, antenna, etc.

(b) The power of each unwanted emission shall be less than TP as specified in the applicable paragraphs listed in the following table:

Transmitter	Emission type	Applicable paragraphs (b)
GMRS	A1D, A3E, F1D, G1D, F3E, G3E with filtering	(1), (3), (7).
	A1D, A3E, F1D, G1D, F3E, G3E without filtering	(5), (6), (7).
	H1D, J1D, R1D, H3E, J3E, R3E	(2), (4), (7).
FRS	F3E with filtering	(1), (3), (7).

R/C:			
	27 MHz	As specified in §95.631(b)	(1), (3), (7).
	72-76 MHz	As specified in §95.631(b)	(1), (3), (7), (10), (11), (12).
CB		A1D, A3E	(1), (3), (8), (9).
		H1D, J1D, R1D, H3E, J3E, R3E	(2), (4), (8), (9).
		A1D, A3E type accepted before September 10, 1976	(1), (3), (7).
		H1D, J1D, R1D, H3E, J3E, R3E type accepted before September 10, 1986	(2), (4), (7).
LPRS		As specified in paragraph (c).	
MedRadio		As specified in paragraph (d).	
DSRCS-OBU		As specified in paragraph (f) of this section.	

(1) At least 25 dB (decibels) on any frequency removed from the center of the authorized bandwidth by more than 50% up to and including 100% of the authorized bandwidth.

(2) At least 25 dB on any frequency removed from the center of the authorized bandwidth by more than 50% up to and including 150% of the authorized bandwidth.

(3) At least 35 dB on any frequency removed from the center of the authorized bandwidth by more than 100% up to and including 250% of the authorized bandwidth.

(4) At least 35 dB on any frequency removed from the center of the authorized bandwidth by more than 150% up to and including 250% of the authorized bandwidth.

(5) At least 83 $\log_{10}$ ($f_d/5$) dB on any frequency removed from the center of the authorized bandwidth by a displacement frequency (f_d in kHz), of more than 5 kHz up to and including 10 kHz.

(6) At least 116 $\log_{10}$ ($f_d/6.1$) dB, or if less, 50 + 10 $\log_{10}$ (T) dB, on any frequency removed from the center of the authorized bandwidth by a displacement frequency (f_d in kHz), of more than 10 kHz up to and including 250% of the authorized bandwidth.

(7) At least 43 + 10 $\log_{10}$ (T) dB on any frequency removed from the center of the authorized bandwidth by more than 250%.

(8) At least 53 + 10 $\log_{10}$ (T) dB on any frequency removed from the center of the authorized bandwidth by more than 250%.

(9) At least 60 dB on any frequency twice or greater than twice the fundamental frequency.

(10) At least 45 dB on any frequency removed from the center of the authorized bandwidth by more than 100% up to and including 125% of the authorized bandwidth.

(11) At least 55 dB on any frequency removed from the center of the authorized bandwidth by more than 125% up to and including 250% of the authorized bandwidth.

(12) At least 56 + 10 $\log_{10}$ (T) dB on any frequency removed from the center of the authorized bandwidth by more than 250%.

(c) For transmitters designed to operate in the LPRS, emissions shall be attenuated in accordance with the following:

(1) Emissions for LPRS transmitters operating on standard band channels (25 kHz) shall be attenuated below the unmodulated carrier in accordance with the following:

(i) Emissions 12.5 kHz to 22.5 kHz away from the channel center frequency: at least 30 dB; and

106

(ii) Emissions more than 22.5 kHz away from the channel center frequency: at least 43 + 10log(carrier power in watts) dB.

(2) Emissions for LPRS transmitters operating on extra band channels (50 kHz) shall be attenuated below the unmodulated carrier in accordance with the following:

(i) Emissions 25 kHz to 35 kHz from the channel center frequency: at least 30 dB; and

(ii) Emissions more than 35 kHz away from the channel center frequency: at least 43 + 10log(carrier power in watts) dB.

(3) Emissions for LPRS transmitters operating on narrowband channels (5 kHz) shall be attenuated below the power (P) of the highest emission, measured in peak values, contained within the authorized bandwidth (4 kHz) in accordance with the following:

(i) On any frequency within the authorized bandwidth: Zero dB;

(ii) On any frequency removed from the center of the authorized bandwidth by a displacement frequency (f_d in kHz) of more than 2 kHz up to and including 3.75 kHz: The lesser of 30 + 20(f_d-2) dB, or 55 + 10 log(P), or 65 dB; and

(iii) On any frequency beyond 3.75 kHz removed from the center of the authorized bandwidth: At least 55 + 10 log(P) dB.

(4) Emissions from AMTS transmitters using a single 250 kHz channel shall be attenuated below the unmodulated carrier in accordance with the following:

(i) Emissions from 125 kHz to 135 kHz away from the channel center frequency; at least 30 dB; and

(ii) Emissions more than 135 kHz away from the channel center frequency; at least 43 + 10log(carrier power in watts) dB.

(d) For transmitters designed to operate in the MedRadio service, emissions shall be attenuated in accordance with the following:

(1) Emissions from a MedRadio transmitter shall be attenuated to a level no greater than the field strength limits shown in the following table when they:

(i) Are more than 250 kHz outside of the 402-405 MHz band (for devices designed to operate in the 402-405 MHz band);

(ii) Are more than 100 kHz outside of either the 401-402 MHz or 405-406 MHz bands (for devices designed to operate in the 401-402 MHz or 405-406 MHz bands);

(iii) Are in the 406.000-406.100 MHz band (for devices designed to operate in the 401-402 MHz or 405-406 MHz bands); or

(iv) Are more than 2.5 MHz outside of the 413-419 MHz, 426-432 MHz, 438-444 MHz, or 451-457 MHz bands (for devices designed to operate in the 413-457 MHz band).

Frequency (MHz)	Field Strength (µV/m)	Measurement Distance (m)
30-88	100	3
88-216	150	3
216-960	200	3
960 and above	500	3

Note—At band edges, the tighter limit applies.

(v) Are more than 2.5 MHz outside of the 2360-2400 MHz band (for devices designed to operate in the 2360-2400 MHz band).

(2) The emission limits shown in the table of paragraph (d)(1) are based on measurements employing a CISPR quasi-peak detector except that above 1 GHz, the limit is based on measurements employing an average detector. Measurements above 1 GHz shall be performed using a minimum resolution bandwidth of 1 MHz. See also §95.605.

(3) The emissions from a MedRadio transmitter must be measured to at least the tenth harmonic of the highest fundamental frequency designed to be emitted by the transmitter.

(4) For devices designed to operate in the 402-405 MHz band: Emissions within the band more than 150 kHz away from the center frequency of the spectrum the transmission is intended to occupy and emissions 250 kHz or less below 402 MHz or above 405 MHz band will be attenuated below the maximum permitted output power by at least 20 dB.

(5) For devices designed to operate in the 401-402 MHz or 405-406 MHz bands: Emissions between 401-401.85 MHz or 405-406 MHz within the MedRadio bands that are more than 50 kHz away from the center frequency of the spectrum the transmission is intended to occupy (or more than 75 kHz away from the center frequency of MedRadio transmitters operating between 401.85-402 MHz) and emissions 100 kHz or less below 401 MHz or above 406 MHz shall be attenuated below the maximum permitted output power by at least 20 dB.

(6) For devices designed to operate in the 413-419 MHz, 426-432 MHz, 438-444 MHz, and 451-457 MHz bands: In the first 2.5 megahertz beyond any of the frequency bands authorized for MMN operation, the EIRP level associated with any unwanted emission must be attenuated within a 1 megahertz bandwidth by at least 20 dB relative to the maximum EIRP level within any 1 megahertz of the fundamental emission.

(7) For devices designed to operate in the 2360-2400 MHz band: In the first 2.5 megahertz beyond any of the frequency bands authorized for MBAN operation, the EIRP level associated with any unwanted emission must be attenuated within a 1

megahertz bandwidth by at least 20 dB relative to the maximum EIRP level within any 1 megahertz of the fundamental emission.

(8) Compliance with the limits described in subparagraphs (4) through (6) are based on the use of measurement instrumentation employing a peak detector function with an instrument resolution bandwidth approximately equal to 1.0 percent of the emission bandwidth of the device under measurement.

(e) For transmitters designed to operate in the MURS, transmitters shall comply with the following:

Frequency	Mask with audio low pass filter	Mask without audio low pass filter
151.820 MHz, 151.880 MHz and 151.940 MHz	(1)	(1)
154.570 MHz and 154.600 MHz	(2)	(3)

(1) *Emission Mask 1*—For transmitters designed to operate with a 12.5 kHz channel bandwidth, any emission must be attenuated below the power (P) of the highest emission contained within the authorized bandwidth as follows:

(i) On any frequency from the center of the authorized bandwidth f_o to 5.625 kHz removed from fo: Zero dB.

(ii) On any frequency removed from the center of the authorized bandwidth by a displacement frequency (f_d in kHz) of more than 5.625 kHz but no more than 12.5 kHz: at least $7.27(f_d-2.88$ kHz) dB.

(iii) On any frequency removed from the center of the authorized bandwidth by a displacement frequency (f_d in kHz) of more than 12.5 kHz: at least 50 + 10 log (P) dB or 70 dB, whichever is the lesser attenuation.

(2) *Emission Mask 2*—For transmitters designed to operate with a 25 kHz channel bandwidth that are equipped with an audio low-pass filter, the power of any emission must be below the unmodulated carrier power (P) as follows:

(i) On any frequency removed from the assigned frequency by more than 50 percent, but not more than 100 percent of the authorized bandwidth: at least 25 dB.

(ii) On any frequency removed from the assigned frequency by more than 100 percent, but not more than 250 percent of the authorized bandwidth: at least 35 dB.

(iii) On any frequency removed from the assigned frequency by more than 250 percent of the authorized bandwidth: at least 43 + 10 log (P) dB.

(3) *Emission Mask 3*—For transmitters designed to operate with a 25 kHz channel bandwidth that are not equipped with an audio low-pass filter, the power of any emission must be attenuated below the unmodulated carrier output power (P) as follows:

(i) On any frequency removed from the center of the authorized bandwidth by a displacement frequency (f_d in kHz) of more than 5 kHz, but not more than 10 kHz: at least 83 log ($f_d/5$) dB.

(ii) On any frequency removed from the center of the authorized bandwidth by a displacement frequency (f_d in kHz) of more than 10 kHz, but not more than 250 percent of the authorized bandwidth: at least 29 log ($f_d^2/11$) dB or 50 dB, whichever is the lesser attenuation.

(iii) On any frequency removed from the center of the authorized bandwidth by more than 250 percent of the authorized bandwidth: at least 43 + 10 log (P) dB.

(f) DSRCS-OBUs are governed under subpart L of this part.

[53 FR 36789, Sept. 22, 1988, as amended at 56 FR 15837, Apr. 18, 1991. Redesignated and amended at 61 FR 28769, 28770, June 6, 1996, and further redesignated and amended at 61 FR 46567, 46568, Sept. 4, 1996; 63 FR 36610, July 7, 1998; 64 FR 69931, Dec. 15, 1999; 65 FR 60878, Oct. 13, 2000; 67 FR 63289, Oct. 11, 2002; 69 FR 46446, Aug. 3, 2004; 74 FR 22707, May 14, 2009; 77 FR 4269, Jan. 27, 2012; 77 FR 55733, Sept. 11, 2012]

§95.637 Modulation standards.

(a) A GMRS transmitter that transmits emission types F1D, G1D, or G3E must not exceed a peak frequency deviation of plus or minus 5 kHz. A GMRS transmitter that transmits emission type F3E must not exceed a peak frequency deviation of plus or minus 5 kHz. A FRS unit that transmits emission type F3E must not exceed a peak frequency deviation of plus or minus 2.5 kHz, and the audio frequency response must not exceed 3.125 kHz .

(b) Each GMRS transmitter, except a mobile station transmitter with a power output of 2.5 W or less, must automatically prevent a greater than normal audio level from causing overmodulation. The transmitter also must include audio frequency low pass filtering, unless it complies with the applicable paragraphs of §95.631 (without filtering.) The filter must be between the modulation limiter and the modulated stage of the transmitter. At any frequency (f in kHz) between 3 and 20 kHz, the filter must have an attenuation of at least 60 $\log_{10}$ (f/3) dB greater than the attenuation at 1 kHz. Above 20 kHz, it must have an attenuation of at least 50 dB greater than the attenuation at 1 kHz.

(c) When emission type A3E is transmitted, the modulation must be greater than 85% but must not exceed 100%. Simultaneous amplitude modulation and frequency or phase modulation of a transmitter are not permitted.

(d) When emission type A3E is transmitted by a CB transmitter having a TP of greater than 2.5 W, the CB transmitter must automatically prevent the modulation from exceeding 100%.

(e) Each CB transmitter that transmits emission type H3E, J3E or R3E must be capable of transmitting the upper sideband. The capability of also transmitting the lower sideband is permitted.

(f) DSRCS-OBUs are governed under subpart L of this part.

[53 FR 36789, Sept. 22, 1988. Redesignated and amended at 61 FR 28769, 28770, June 6, 1996, and further redesignated at 61 FR 46567, Sept. 4, 1996; 69 FR 46446, Aug. 3, 2004]

§95.639 Maximum transmitter power.

(a) No GMRS transmitter, under any condition of modulation, shall exceed:

(1) 50 W *Carrier power* (average TP during one unmodulated RF cycle) when transmitting emission type A1D, F1D, G1D, A3E, F3E or G3E.

(2) 50 W peak envelope TP when transmitting emission type H1D, J1D, R1D, H3E, J3E or R3E.

(b) No R/C transmitter, under any condition of modulation, shall exceed a carrier power or peak envelope TP (single-sideband only) of:

(1) 4 W in the 26-27 MHz frequency band, except on channel frequency 27.255 MHz;

(2) 25 W on channel frequency 27.255 MHz;

(3) 0.75 W in the 72-76 MHz frequency band.

(c) No CB transmitter, under any condition of modulation, shall exceed:

(1) 4 W Carrier power when transmitting emission type A1D or A3E;

(2) 12 W peak envelope TP when transmitting emission type H1D, J1D, R1D, H3E, J3E or R3E. Each CB transmitter which transmits emission type H3E, J3E or R3E must automatically prevent the TP from exceeding 12 W peak envelope TP or the manufacturer's rated peak envelope TP, whichever is less.

(d) No FRS unit, under any condition of modulation, shall exceed 0.500 W effective radiated power (ERP).

(e) The maximum transmitter output power authorized for LPRS stations is 100 mW.

(f) In the MedRadio Service:

(1) For transmitters operating in the 401-406 MHz band that are not excepted under §95.627(b) from the frequency monitoring requirements of §95.627(a), the maximum radiated power in any 300 kHz bandwidth by MedRadio transmitters operating at 402-405 MHz, or in any 100 kHz bandwidth by MedRadio transmitters operating at 401-402 MHz or 405-406 MHz shall not exceed 25 microwatts EIRP. For transmitters that are excepted under §95.627(b) from the frequency monitoring requirements of §95.627(a), the power radiated by any station operating in 402-405 MHz shall not exceed 100 nanowatts EIRP confined to a maximum total emission bandwidth of 300 kHz centered at 403.65 MHz, the power radiated by any station operating in 401-401.85 MHz or 405-406 MHz shall not exceed 250 nanowatts EIRP in any 100 kHz bandwidth and the power radiated by any station operating in 401.85-402 MHz shall not exceed 25 microwatts in the 150 kHz bandwidth. See §§95.633(e).

(2) For transmitters operating in 413-419 MHz, 426-432 MHz, 438-444 MHz, or 451-457 MHz bands, the peak EIRP over the frequency bands of operation shall not exceed the lesser of 1 mW or 10 log B—7.782 dBm, where B is the 20 dB emission bandwidth in MHz; and the peak power spectral density shall not exceed 800 microwatts per megahertz in any 1 megahertz band.

(3) For transmitters operating in the 2360-2390 MHz band, the maximum EIRP over the frequency bands of operation shall not exceed the lesser of 1 mW or 10*log (B) dBm, where B is the 20 dB emission bandwidth in MHz.

(4) For transmitters operating in the 2390-2400 MHz band, the maximum EIRP over the frequency bands of operation shall

not exceed the lesser of 20 mW or 16+10*log (B) dBm, where B is the 20 dB emission bandwidth in MHz.

(5) The antenna associated with any MedRadio transmitter must be supplied with the transmitter and shall be considered part of the transmitter subject to equipment authorization. Compliance with these EIRP limits may be determined as set forth in §95.627(g) or §95.628(h), as applicable.

(g) The maximum field strength authorized for WMTS stations in the 608-614 MHz band is 200 mV/m, measured at 3 meters. For stations in the 1395-1400 MHz and 1427-1429.5 MHz bands, the maximum field strength is 740 mV/m, measured at 3 meters.

(h) No MURS unit, under any condition of modulation, shall exceed 2 Watts transmitter power output.

(i) DSRCS-OBUs are governed under subpart L of this part, except the maximum output power for portable DSRCS-OBUs is 1.0 mW. For purposes of this paragraph, a portable is a transmitting device designed to be used so that the radiating structure(s) of the device is/are within 20 centimeters of the body of the user.

[53 FR 36789, Sept. 22, 1988; 53 FR 44144, Nov. 1, 1988. Redesignated at 61 FR 28769, 28770, June 6, 1996, and further redesignated at 61 FR 46567, 46569, Sept. 4, 1996]

EDITORIAL NOTE: For FEDERAL REGISTER citations affecting §95.639, see the List of CFR Sections Affected, which appears in the Finding Aids section of the printed volume and at *www.fdsys.gov*.

CERTIFICATION REQUIREMENTS

§95.643 DSRCS-OBU certification.

Sections 95.645 through 95.655 do not apply to certification of DSRCS-OBUs. DSRCS-OBUs must be certified in accordance with subpart L of this part and subpart J of part 2 of this chapter.

[69 FR 46446, Aug. 3, 2004]

§95.645 Control accessibility.

(a) No control, switch or other type of adjustment which, when manipulated, can result in a violation of the rules shall be accessible from the transmitter operating panel or from exterior of the transmitter enclosure.

(b) An R/C transmitter which incorporates plug-in frequency determining modules which are changed by the user must be certificated with the modules. Each module must contain all of the frequency determining circuitry including the oscillator. Plug-in crystals are not considered modules and must not be accessible to the user.

[53 FR 36789, Sept. 22, 1988. Redesignated at 61 FR 28769, June 6, 1996, and further redesignated at 61 FR 46567, Sept. 4, 1996; 63 FR 36610, July 7, 1998]

§95.647 FRS unit and R/C transmitter antennas.

The antenna of each FRS unit, and the antenna of each R/C station transmitting in the 72-76 MHz band, must be an integral part of the transmitter. The antenna must have no gain (as compared to a half-wave dipole) and must be vertically polarized.

[61 FR 28770, June 6, 1996. Redesignated at 61 FR 46567, Sept. 4, 1996]

§95.649 Power capability.

No CB, R/C, LPRS, FRS, MedRadio, MURS, or WMTS unit shall incorporate provisions for increasing its transmitter power to any level in excess of the limits specified in §95.639.

[74 FR 22708, May 14, 2009]

§95.651 Crystal control required.

All transmitters used in the Personal Radio Services must be crystal controlled, except an R/C station that transmits in the 26-27 MHz frequency band, a FRS unit, a LPRS unit, a MURS unit, a MedRadio transmitter, or a WMTS unit.

[74 FR 22708, May 14, 2009]

§95.653 Instructions and warnings.

(a) A user's instruction manual must be supplied with each transmitter marketed, and one copy (a draft or preliminary copy is acceptable provided a final copy is provided when completed) must be forwarded to the FCC with each request for certification.

(b) The instruction manual must contain all information necessary for the proper installation and operation of the transmitter including:

(1) Instructions concerning all controls, adjustments and switches that may be operated or adjusted without resulting in a violation of the rules.

(2) Warnings concerning any adjustment that could result in a violation of the rules or that is recommended to be performed by or under the immediate supervision and responsibility of a person certified as technically qualified to perform transmitter maintenance and repair duties in the private land mobile services and fixed services by an organization or committee representative of users of those services.

(3) Warnings concerning the replacement of any transmitter component (crystal, semiconductor, etc.) that could result in a violation of the rules.

(4) For a CMRS transmitter, warnings concerning licensing requirements and information concerning license application procedures.

[53 FR 36789, Sept. 22, 1988. Redesignated at 61 FR 28769, June 6, 1996, and further redesignated at 61 FR 46567, Sept. 4, 1996; 63 FR 36610, July 7, 1998]

§95.655 Frequency capability.

(a) No transmitter will be certificated for use in the CB service if it is equipped with a frequency capability not listed in §95.625, and no transmitter will be certificated for use in the GMRS if it is equipped with a frequency capability not listed in §95.621, unless such transmitter is also certificated for use in another radio service for which the frequency is authorized and for which certification is also required. (Transmitters with frequency capability for the Amateur Radio Services and Military Affiliate Radio System will not be certificated.)

(b) All frequency determining circuitry (including crystals) and programming controls in each CB transmitter and in each GMRS transmitter must be internal to the transmitter and must not be accessible from the exterior of the transmitter operating panel or from the exterior of the transmitter enclosure.

(c) No add-on device, whether internal or external, the function of which is to extend the transmitting frequency capability of a CB transmitter beyond its original capability, shall be manufactured, sold or attached to any CB station transmitter.

(d) No transmitter will be certificated for use in MURS if it is equipped with a frequency capability not listed in §95.632.

[53 FR 47718, Nov. 25, 1988. Redesignated at 61 FR 28769, June 6, 1996, and further redesignated at 61 FR 46567, Sept. 4, 1996 and amended at 63 FR 36611, July 7, 1998; 67 FR 63290, Oct. 11, 2002; 69 FR 32886, June 14, 2004]

ADDITIONAL CERTIFICATION REQUIREMENTS FOR CB TRANSMITTERS

§95.665 [Reserved]

§95.667 CB transmitter power.

The dissipation rating of all the semiconductors or electron tubes which supply RF power to the antenna terminals of each CB transmitter must not exceed 10 W. For semiconductors, the dissipation rating is the greater of the collector or device dissipation value established by the manufacturer of the semiconductor. These values may be temperature de-rated by no more than 50 °C. For an electron tube, the dissipation rating is the Intermittent Commercial and Amateur Service plate dissipation value established by the manufacturer of the electron tube.

[53 FR 36789, Sept. 22, 1988. Redesignated at 61 FR 28769, June 6, 1996, and further redesignated at 61 FR 46567, Sept. 4, 1996]

§95.669 External controls.

(a) Only the following external transmitter controls, connections or devices will normally be permitted in a CB transmitter:

(1) Primary power connection. (Circuitry or devices such as rectifiers, transformers, or inverters which provide the nominal rated transmitter primary supply voltage may be used without voiding the transmitter certification.)

(2) Microphone connection.

(3) Antenna terminals.

(4) Audio frequency power amplifier output connector and selector switch.

(5) On-off switch for primary power to transmitter. This switch may be combined with receiver controls such as the receiver on-off switch and volume control.

(6) Upper/lower sideband selector switch (for a transmitter that transmits emission type H3E, J3E or R3E).

(7) Carrier level selector control (for a transmitter that transmits emission type H3E, J3E or R3E.) This control may be combined with the sideband selector switch.

(8) Channel frequency selector switch.

(9) Transmit/receive selector switch.

(10) Meter(s) and selector switch(es) for monitoring transmitter performance.

(11) Pilot lamp(s) or meter(s) to indicate the presence of RF output power or that the transmitter control circuits are activated to transmit.

(b) The FCC may authorize additional controls, connections or devices after considering the functions to be performed by such additions.

[53 FR 36789, Sept. 22, 1988. Redesignated at 61 FR 28769, June 6, 1996, and further redesignated at 61 FR 46567, Sept. 4, 1996; 63 FR 36611, July 7, 1998]

§95.671 Serial number.

The serial number of each CB transmitter must be engraved on the transmitter chassis.

[53 FR 36789, Sept. 22, 1988. Redesignated at 61 FR 28769, June 6, 1996, and further redesignated at 61 FR 46567, Sept. 4, 1996]

§95.673 Copy of rules.

A copy of part 95, subpart D, of the FCC Rules, current at the time of packing of the transmitter, must be furnished with each CB transmitter marketed.

[53 FR 36789, Sept. 22, 1988. Redesignated at 61 FR 28769, June 6, 1996, and further redesignated at 61 FR 46567, Sept. 4, 1996]

Appendix 1 to Subpart E of Part 95—Glossary of Terms

The definitions used in this subpart E are:

Authorized bandwidth. Maximum permissible bandwidth of a transmission.

Carrier power. Average TP during one unmodulated RF cycle.

CB. Citizens Band Radio Service.

CB transmitter. A transmitter that operates or is intended to operate at a station authorized in the CB.

Channel frequencies. Reference frequencies from which the carrier frequency, suppressed or otherwise, may not deviate by more than the specified frequency tolerance.

Crystal. Quartz piezo-electric element.

Crystal controlled. Use of a crystal to establish the transmitted frequency.

dB. Decibels.

EIRP. Effective Isotropic Radiated Power. Antenna input power times gain for free-space or in-tissue measurement configurations required by MedRadio, expressed in watts, where the gain is referenced to an isotropic radiator.

FCC. Federal Communications Commission.

Filtering. Refers to the requirement in §95.633(b).

FRS. Family Radio Service.

GMRS. General Mobile Radio Service.

GMRS transmitter. A transmitter that operates or is intended to operate at a station authorized in the GMRS.

Harmful interference. Any transmission, radiation or induction that endangers the functioning of a radio navigation or other safety service or seriously degrades, obstructs or repeatedly interrupts a radio communication service operating in accordance with applicable laws, treaties and regulations.

Mean power. TP averaged over at least 30 cycles of the lowest modulating frequency, typically 0.1 seconds at maximum power.

Medical Body Area Network (MBAN). An MBAN is a low power network consisting of a MedRadio programmer/control transmitter and multiple medical body-worn devices all of which transmit or receive non-voice data or related device control commands for the purpose of measuring and recording physiological parameters and other patient information or performing diagnostic or therapeutic functions via radiated bi- or uni-directional electromagnetic signals.

Medical body-worn device. Apparatus that is placed on or in close proximity to the human body (e.g., within a few centimeters) for the purpose of performing diagnostic or therapeutic functions.

Medical body-worn transmitter. A MedRadio transmitter intended to be placed on or in close proximity to the human body (e.g., within a few centimeters) used to facilitate communications with other medical communications devices for purposes of delivering medical therapy to a patient or collecting medical diagnostic information from a patient.

Medical implant device. Apparatus that is placed inside the human body for the purpose of performing diagnostic or therapeutic functions.

Medical implant event. An occurrence or the lack of an occurrence recognized by a medical implant device, or a duly authorized health care professional, that requires the transmission of data from a medical implant transmitter in order to protect the safety or well-being of the person in whom the medical implant transmitter has been implanted.

Medical implant transmitter. A MedRadio transmitter in which both the antenna and transmitter device are designed to operate within a human body for the purpose of facilitating communications from a medical implant device.

Medical Micropower Network (MMN). An ultra-low power wideband network consisting of a MedRadio programmer/control transmitter and medical implant transmitters, all of which transmit or receive non-voice data or related device control commands for the purpose of facilitating functional electric stimulation, a technique using electric currents to activate and monitor nerves and muscles.

MedRadio programmer/control transmitter. A MedRadio transmitter that operates or is designed to operate outside of a human body for the purpose of communicating with a receiver, or for triggering a transmitter, connected to a medical implant device or to a medical body-worn device used in the MedRadio Service; and which also typically includes a frequency monitoring system that initiates a MedRadio communications session.

MedRadio Service. Medical Device Radio communication Service.

MedRadio transmitter. A transmitter authorized to operate in the MedRadio service.

MURS. Multi-Use Radio Service.

Peak envelope power. TP averaged during one RF cycle at the highest crest of the modulation envelope.

R/C. Radio Control Radio Service.

R/C transmitter. A transmitter that operates or is intended to operate at a station authorized in the R/C.

126

RF. Radio frequency.

TP. RF transmitter power expressed in W, either mean or peak envelope, as measured at the transmitter output antenna terminals.

Transmitter. Apparatus that converts electrical energy received from a source into RF energy capable of being radiated.

W. Watts.

[65 FR 60878, Oct. 13, 2000, as amended at 74 FR 22708, May 14, 2009; 77 FR 4269, Jan. 27, 2012; 77 FR 55733, Sept. 11, 2012]

Subpart F—218-219 MHz Service

GENERAL PROVISIONS

SOURCE: 57 FR 8275, Mar. 9, 1992, unless otherwise noted.

§95.801 Scope.

This subpart sets out the regulations governing the licensing and operation of a 218-219 MHz system. This subpart supplements part 1, subpart F of this chapter, which establishes the requirements and conditions under which commercial and private radio stations may be licensed and used in the Wireless Telecommunications Services. The provisions of this subpart contain additional pertinent information for current and prospective licensees specific to the services governed by this part 95.

[64 FR 59659, Nov. 3, 1999]

§95.803 218-219MHz Service description.

(a) The 218-219 MHz Service is authorized for system licensees to provide communication service to subscribers in a specific service area.

(b) The components of each 218-219 MHz Service system are its administrative apparatus, its response transmitter units (RTUs), and one or more cell transmitter stations (CTSs). RTUs may be used in any location within the service area. CTSs provide service from a fixed point, and certain CTSs must be individually licensed as part of a 218-219 MHz Service system. See §95.811.

(c) Each 218-219 MHz Service system service area is one of the cellular system service areas as defined by the Commission, unless modified pursuant to §95.823.

[66 FR 9218, Apr. 9, 2001]

§95.805 Permissible communications.

A 218-219 MHz Service system may provide any fixed or mobile communications service to subscribers within its service area on its assigned spectrum, consistent with the Commission's rules and the regulatory status of the system to provide services on a common carrier or private basis.

[64 FR 59660, Nov. 3, 1999]

§95.807 Requesting regulatory status.

(a) Authorizations for systems in the 218-219 MHz Service will be granted to provide services on a common carrier basis or a private (non-common carrier and/or private internal-use) basis.

(1) *Initial applications.* An applicant will specify on FCC Form 601 if it is requesting authorizations to provide services on a common carrier, non-common carrier or private internal-use basis, of a combination thereof.

(2) *Amendment of pending applications.* Any pending application may be amended to:

(i) Change the carrier status requested; or

(ii) Add to the pending request in order to obtain both common carrier and private status in a single license.

(3) *Modification of license.* A licensee may modify a license to:

(i) Change the carrier status authorized; or

(ii) Add to the status authorized in order to obtain both common carrier and private status in a single license. Applications to change, or add to, carrier status in a license must be submitted on FCC Form 601 in accordance with §1.1102 of this chapter.

(4) *Pre-existing licenses.* Licenses granted before April 9, 2001. are authorized to provide services on a private (non-common carrier) basis. Licensees may modify this initial status pursuant to paragraph (a)(3) of this section.

(b) An applicant or licensee may submit a petition at any time requesting clarification of the regulatory status required to provide a specific communications service.

[64 FR 59660, Nov. 3, 1999, as amended at 66 FR 9219, Feb. 7, 2001]

SYSTEM LICENSE REQUIREMENTS

§95.811 License requirements.

(a) Each 218-219 MHz Service system must be licensed in accordance with part 1, subpart F of this chapter.

(b) Each CTS where the antenna does not exceed 6.1 meters (20 feet) above ground or an existing structure (other than an antenna structure) and is outside the vicinity of certain receiving locations (see §1.924 of this chapter) is authorized under the 218-219 MHz System license. All other CTS must be individually licensed.

(c) All CTSs not meeting the licensing criteria under paragraph (b) of this section are authorized under the 218-219 MHz Service system license.

(d) Each component RTU in a 218-219 MHz Service system is authorized under the system license or if associated with an individually licensed CTS, under that CTS license.

(e) Each CTS (regardless of whether it is individually licensed) and each RTU must be in compliance with the Commission's environmental rules (see part 1, subpart I of this chapter) and the Commission's rules pertaining to the construction, marking and lighting of antenna structures (see part 17 of this chapter).

[57 FR 8275, Mar. 9, 1992, as amended at 57 FR 36373, Aug. 13, 1992; 63 FR 68977, Dec. 14, 1998; 64 FR 59660, Nov. 3, 1999; 66 FR 9219, Feb. 7, 2001]

§95.812 License term.

(a) The term of each 218-219 MHz service system license is ten years from the date of original grant or renewal.

(b) Licenses for individually licensed CTSs will be issued for a period running concurrently with the license of the associated 218-219 MHz Service system with which it is licensed.

[64 FR 59660, Nov. 3, 1999, as amended at 66 FR 9219, Feb. 7, 2001]

§95.813 Eligibility.

(a) An entity is eligible to hold a 218-219 MHz Service system license and its associated individual CTS licenses if:

(1) The entity is an individual who is not a representative of a foreign government; or

(2) The entity is a partnership and no partner is a representative of a foreign government; or

(3) The entity is a corporation organized under the laws of the United States of America; or

(4) The entity is a trust and no beneficiary is a representative of a foreign government.

(b) An entity that loses its 218-219 MHz Service authorization due to failure to meet the construction requirements specified in §95.833 of this part may not apply for a 218-219 MHz Service system license for three years from the date the Commission takes final action affirming that the 218-219 MHz Service license has been canceled.

[57 FR 8275, Mar. 9, 1992, as amended at 58 FR 25952, Apr. 29, 1993; 64 FR 59660, Nov. 3, 1999]

§95.815 License application.

(a) In addition to the requirements of part 1, subpart F of this chapter, each application for a 218-219 MHz Service system license must include a plan analyzing the co- and adjacent channel interference potential of the proposed system, identifying methods being used to minimize this interference, and showing how the proposed system will meet the service requirements set forth in §95.831 of this part. This plan must be updated to reflect changes to the 218-219 MHz Service system design or construction.

(b) In addition to the requirements of part 1, subpart F of this chapter, each request by a 218-219 MHz Service system licensee to add, delete, or modify technical information of an individually licensed CTS (*see* §95.811(b) of this part) must include a description of the system after the proposed addition, deletion, or modifications, including the population in the service area, the number of component CTSs, and an explanation of how the system will satisfy the service requirements specified in §95.831 of this part.

[63 FR 68977, Dec. 14, 1998, as amended at 64 FR 59660, Nov. 3, 1999]

§95.816 Competitive bidding proceedings.

(a) Mutually exclusive initial applications for 218-219 MHz Service licenses are subject to competitive bidding. The general competitive bidding procedures set forth in part 1, subpart Q of this chapter will apply unless otherwise provided in this part.

(b) *Installment payments.* Eligible Licensees that elect resumption pursuant to Amendment of part 95 of the Commission's Rules to Provide Regulatory Flexibility in the 218-219 MHz Service, *Report and Order and Memorandum Opinion and Order,* FCC 99-239 (released September 10, 1999) may continue to participate in the installment payment program. Eligible Licensees are those that were current in installment payments (*i.e.* less than ninety days delinquent) as of March 16, 1998, or those that had properly filed grace period requests under the former installment payment rules. All unpaid interest from grant date through election date will be capitalized into the principal as of Election Day creating a new principal amount. Installment payments must be made on a quarterly basis. Installment payments will be calculated based on new principal amount as of Election Day and will fully amortize over the remaining term of the license. The interest rate will equal the rate for five-year U.S. Treasury obligations at the grant date.

(c) *Eligibility for small business provisions.* (1) A small business is an entity that, together with its affiliates and controlling interests, has average gross revenues not to exceed $15 million for the preceding three years.

(2) A very small business is an entity that, together with its affiliates and controlling interests, has average gross revenues not to exceed $3 million for the preceding three years.

(d) *Bidding credits.* A winning bidder that qualifies as a small business, as defined in this subsection, or a consortium of small businesses may use the bidding credit specified in §1.2110(f)(2)(ii) of this chapter. A winning bidder that qualifies as a very small business, as defined in this section, or a consortium of very small businesses may use the bidding credit specified in accordance with §1.2110(f)(2)(i) of this chapter.

(e) Winning bidders in Auction No. 2, which took place on July 28-29, 1994, that, at the time of auction, met the qualifications under the Commission's rules then in effect, for small business status will receive a twenty-five percent bidding credit pursuant to Amendment of part 95 of the Commission's Rules to Provide Regulatory Flexibility in the 218-219 MHz Service, Report and Order and Memorandum Opinion and Order, FCC 99-239 (released September 10, 1999).

[64 FR 59660, Nov. 3, 1999, as amended at 66 FR 9219, Feb. 7, 2001; 67 FR 45378, July 9, 2002; 68 FR 43001, July 21, 2003]

§95.819 License transferability.

(a) A 218-219 MHz Service system license, together with all of its component CTS licenses, may be transferred, assigned, sold, or given away only in accordance with the provisions and procedures set forth in §1.948 of this chapter. For licenses acquired through competitive bidding procedures (including licenses obtained in cases of no mutual exclusivity), designated entities must comply with §§1.2110 and 1.2111 of this chapter (see §1.948(a)(3) of this chapter).

(b) If the transfer, assignment, sale, or gift of a license is approved, the new licensee is held to the construction requirements set forth in §95.833.

[66 FR 9219, Feb. 7, 2001]

§95.823 Geographic partitioning and spectrum disaggregation.

(a) *Eligibility.* Parties seeking Commission approval of geographic partitioning or spectrum disaggregation of 218-219 MHz Service system licenses shall request an authorization for partial assignment of license pursuant to §1.948 of this chapter.

(b) *Technical standards—*(1) *Partitioning.* In the case of partitioning, requests for authorization of partial assignment of a license must include, as attachments, a description of the partitioned service area and a calculation of the population of the partitioned service area and the licensed geographic service area. The partitioned service area shall be defined by coordinate points at every 3 seconds along the partitioned service area unless an FCC-recognized service area (*i.e.* Economic Areas) is utilized or county lines are followed. The geographic coordinates must be specified in degrees, minutes, and seconds, to the nearest second of latitude and longitude, and must be based upon the 1983 North American Datum (NAD83). In the case where an FCC-recognized service area or county lines are utilized, applicants need only list the specific area(s) (through use of FCC designations or county names) that constitute the partitioned area.

(2) *Disaggregation.* Spectrum maybe disaggregated in any amount.

(3) *Combined partitioning and disaggregation.* The Commission will consider requests for partial assignments of licenses that propose combinations of partitioning and disaggregation.

(c) *Provisions applicable to designated entities*—(1) *Parties not qualified for installment payment plans.* (i) When a winning bidder (partitionor or disaggregator) that elected to pay for its license through an installment payment plan partitions its license or disaggregates spectrum to another party (partitionee or disaggregatee) that would not qualify for an installment payment plan, or elects not to pay for its share of the license through installment payments, the outstanding principal balance owed by the partitionor or disaggregator shall be apportioned according to §1.2111(e)(3) of this chapter. The partitionor or disaggregator is responsible for accrued and unpaid interest through and including the consummation date.

(ii) The partitionee or disaggregatee shall, as a condition of the approval of the partial assignment application, pay its entire *pro rata* amount of the outstanding principal balance on or before the consummation date. Failure to meet this condition will result in cancellation of the grant of the partial assignment application.

(iii) The partitionor or disaggregator shall be permitted to continue to pay its pro rata share of the outstanding balance and, if applicable, shall receive loan documents evidencing the partitioning and disaggregation. The original interest rate, established pursuant to §1.2110(g)(3)(i) of this chapter at the time of the grant of the initial license in the market, shall continue to be applied to the partitionor's or disaggregator's portion of the remaining government obligation.

(iv) A default on the partitionor's or disaggregator's payment obligation will affect only the partitionor's or disaggregator's portion of the market.

(2) Parties qualified for installment payment plans.

(i) Where both parties to a partitioning or disaggregation agreement qualify for installment payments, the partitionee or disaggregatee will be permitted to make installment payments on its portion of the remaining government obligation.

(ii) Each party may be required, as a condition to approval of the partial assignment application, to execute loan documents agreeing to pay its *pro rata* portion of the outstanding principal balance due, as apportioned according to §1.2111(e)(3) of this chapter, based upon the installment payment terms for which it qualifies under the rules. Failure by either party to meet this condition will result in the automatic cancellation of the grant of the partial assignment application. The interest rate, established pursuant to §1.2110(f)(3)(i) of this chapter at the time of the grant of the initial license in the market, shall continue to be applied to both parties' portion of the balance due. Each party will receive a license for its portion of the partitioned market.

(iii) A default on an obligation will affect only that portion of the market area held by the defaulting party.

(d) *Construction requirements*—(1) *Partitioning.* Partial assignors and assignees for license partitioning have two options to meet construction requirements. Under the first option, the partitionor and partitionee would each certify that they will independently satisfy the applicable construction requirements set forth in §95.833 of this part for their respective partitioned areas. If either licensee failed to meet its requirement in §95.833 of this part, only the non-performing licensee's renewal application would be subject to dismissal. Under the second option, the partitionor certifies that it has met or will meet the requirement in §95.833 of this part for the entire market. If the partitionor fails to meet the requirement in §95.833 of this part, however, only its renewal application would be subject to forfeiture at renewal.

(2) *Disaggregation.* Partial assignors and assignees for license disaggregation have two options to meet construction requirements. Under the first option, the disaggregator and disaggregatee would certify that they each will share responsibility for meeting the applicable construction requirements set forth in §95.833 of this part for the geographic service area. If parties choose this option and either party fails to do so, both licenses would be subject to forfeiture at renewal. The second option would allow the parties to agree that either the disaggregator or the disaggregatee would be responsible for meeting the requirement in §95.833 of this part for the geographic service area. If parties choose this option, and the party responsible for meeting the construction requirement fails

to do so, only the license of the non-performing party would be subject to forfeiture at renewal.

(3) All applications requesting partial assignments of license for partitioning or disaggregation must include the above-referenced certification as to which of the construction options is selected.

(4) Responsible parties must submit supporting documents showing compliance with the respective construction requirements within the appropriate construction benchmarks set forth in §95.833 of this part.

[64 FR 59662, Nov. 3, 1999, as amended at 67 FR 46378, July 9, 2002]

SYSTEM REQUIREMENTS

§95.831 Service requirements.

Subject to the initial construction requirements of §95.833 of this subpart, each 218-219 MHz Service system license must demonstrate that it provides substantial service within the service area. Substantial service is defined as a service that is sound, favorable, and substantially above a level of service which might minimally warrant renewal.

[64 FR 59662, Nov. 3, 1999]

§95.833 Construction requirements.

(a) Each 218-219 MHz Service licensee must make a showing of "substantial service" within ten years of the license grant. A "substantial service" assessment will be made at renewal pursuant to the provisions and procedures contained in §1.949 of this chapter.

(b) Each 218-219 MHz Service licensee must file a report to be submitted to inform the Commission of the service status of its system. The report must be labeled as an exhibit to the renewal application. At minimum, the report must include:

(1) A description of its current service in terms of geographic coverage and population served;

(2) An explanation of its record of expansion, including a timetable of new construction to meet changes in demand for service;

(3) A description of its investments in its 218-219 MHz Service systems;

(4) A list, including addresses, of all component CTSs constructed; and

(5) Copies of all FCC orders finding the licensee to have violated the Communications Act or any FCC rule or policy; and a list of any pending proceedings that relate to any matter described in this paragraph.

(c) Failure to demonstrate that substantial service is being provided in the service area will result in forfeiture of the license, and will result in the licensee's ineligibility to apply for 218-219 MHz Service licenses for three years from the date the Commission takes final action affirming that the 218-219 MHz Service license has been canceled pursuant to §95.813 of this part.

[64 FR 59662, Nov. 3, 1999]

§95.835 Station identification.

No RTU or CTS is required to transmit a station identification announcement.

§95.837 Station inspection.

Upon request by an authorized Commission representative, the 218-219 MHz Service system licensee must make any component CTS available for inspection.

TECHNICAL STANDARDS

§95.851 Certification.

Each CTS and RTU transmitter must be certificated for use in the 218-219 MHz Service in accordance with subpart J of part 2 of this chapter.

[63 FR 36611, July 7, 1998]

§95.853 Frequency segments.

There are two frequency segments available for assignment to the 218-219 MHz Service in each service area. Frequency segment A is 218.000-218.500 MHz. Frequency segment B is 218.501-219.000 MHz.

[64 FR 59663, Nov. 3, 1999]

§95.855 Transmitter effective radiated power limitation.

The effective radiated power (ERP) of each CTS and RTU shall be limited to the minimum necessary for successful communications. No CTS or fixed RTU may transmit with an ERP exceeding 20 watts. No mobile RTU may transmit with an ERP exceeding 4 watts.

[64 FR 59663, Nov. 3, 1999]

§95.857 Emission standards.

(a) All transmissions by each CTS and by each RTU shall use an emission type that complies with the following standard for unnecessary radiation.

(b) All spurious and out-of-band emissions shall be attenuated:

(1) Zero dB on any frequency within the authorized frequency segment.

(2) At least 28 dB on any frequency removed from the midpoint of the assigned frequency segment by more than 250 kHz up to and including 750 kHz;

(3) At least 35 dB on any frequency removed from the midpoint of the assigned frequency segment by more than 750 kHz up to and including 1250 kHz;

(4) At least 43 plus 10 log (base 10) (mean power in watts) dB on any frequency removed from the midpoint of the assigned frequency segment by more than 1250 kHz.

(c) When testing for certification, all measurements of unnecessary radiation are performed using a carrier frequency as close to the edge of the authorized frequency segment as the transmitter is designed to be capable of operating.

(d) The resolution bandwidth of the instrumentation used to measure the emission power shall be 100 Hz for measuring emissions up to and including 250 kHz from the edge of the authorized frequency segment, and 10 kHz for measuring emissions more than 250 kHz from the edge of the authorized frequency segment. If a video filter is used, its bandwidth shall not be less than the resolution bandwidth. The power level of the highest emission within the frequency segment, to which the attenuation is referenced, shall be remeasured for each change in resolution bandwidth.

[57 FR 8275, Mar. 9, 1992, as amended at 63 FR 36611, July 7, 1998]

§95.859 Antennas.

(a) The overall height from ground to topmost tip of the CTS antenna shall not exceed the height necessary to assure adequate service. Certain CTS antennas must be individually licensed to the 218-219 MHz System licensee (see §95.811(b) of this part) and the antenna structures of which they are a part must be registered with the Commission (*see* part 17 of this chapter).

(b) [Reserved]

(c) The RTU may be connected to an external antenna not more than 6.1 m (20 feet) above ground or above an existing man-made structure (other than an antenna structure). Connectors that are used to connect RTUs to an external antenna shall not be of the types generally known as "F-type" or "BNC type." Use of an external antenna is subject to §95.861.

[57 FR 36373, Aug. 13, 1992, as amended at 64 FR 59663, Nov. 3, 1999]

§95.861 Interference.

(a) When a 218-219 MHz Service system suffers harmful interference within its service area or causes harmful interference to another 218-219 MHz Service system, the licensees of both systems must cooperate and resolve the problem by mutually satisfactory arrangements. If the licensees are unable to do so, the Commission may impose restrictions including, but not limited to, specifying the transmitter power, antenna height or area, duty cycle, or hours of operation for the stations concerned.

(b) The use of any frequency segment (or portion thereof) at a given geographical location may be denied when, in the judgment of the Commission, its use in that location is not in the public interest; the use of a frequency segment (or portion thereof) specified for the 218-219 MHz Service system may be restricted as to specified geographical areas, maximum power, or other operating conditions.

(c) A 218-219 MHz Service licensee must provide a copy of the plan required by §95.815 (a) of this part to every TV Channel 13 station whose Grade B predicted contour overlaps the licensed service area for the 218-219 MHz Service system. The 218-219 MHz Service licensee must send the plan to the TV Channel 13 licensee(s) within 10 days from the date the 218-219 MHz Service submits the plan to the Commission, and the 218-219 MHz Service licensee must send updates to this plan to the

TV Channel 13 licensee(s) within 10 days from the date that such updates are filed with the Commission pursuant to §95.815.

(d) Each 218-219 MHz Service system licensee must provide upon request, and install free of charge, an interference reduction device to any household within a TV Channel 13 station Grade B predicted contour that experiences interference due to a component CTS or RTU.

(e) Each 218-219 MHz Service system licensee must investigate and eliminate harmful interference to television broadcasting and reception, from its component CTSs and RTSs, within 30 days of the time it is notified in writing, by either an affected television station, an affected viewer, or the Commission, of an interference complaint. Should the licensee fail to eliminate the interference within the 30-day period, the CTS(s) or RTU(s) causing the problem(s) must discontinue operation.

(f) The boundary of the 218-219 MHz Service system, as defined in its authorization, is the limit of interference protection for that 218-219 MHz Service system.

[64 FR 59663, Nov. 3, 1999, as amended at 66 FR 9219, Feb. 7, 2001]

Subpart G—Low Power Radio Service (LPRS)

SOURCE: 61 FR 46569, Sept. 4, 1996, unless otherwise noted.

GENERAL PROVISIONS

§95.1001 Eligibility.

An entity is authorized by rule to operate a LPRS transmitter and is not required to be individually licensed by the FCC if it is not a representative of a foreign government and if it uses the transmitter only in accordance with §95.1009. Each entity operating a LPRS transmitter for AMTS purposes must hold an AMTS license under part 80 of this chapter.

§95.1003 Authorized locations.

LPRS operation is authorized:

(a) Anywhere CB station operation is permitted under §95.405(a); and

(b) Aboard any vessel or aircraft of the United States, with the permission of the captain, while the vessel or aircraft is either travelling domestically or in international waters or airspace.

(c) Anyone intending to operate an LPRS transmitter on the islands of Puerto Rico, Desecheo, Mona, Vieques, and Culebra in a manner that could pose an interference threat to the Arecibo Observatory shall notify the Interference Office, Arecibo Observatory, HC3 Box 53995, Arecibo, Puerto Rico 00612, in writing or electronically, of the location of the unit. Operators may wish to consult interference guidelines, which will be provided by Cornell University. Operators who choose to transmit information electronically should e-mail to: *prcz@naic.edu.*

(1) The notification to the Interference Office, Arecibo Observatory shall be made 45 days prior to commencing

operation of the transmitter. The notification shall state the geographical coordinates of the unit.

(2) After receipt of such notifications, the Commission will allow the Arecibo Observatory a period of 20 days for comments or objections. The operator will be required to make reasonable efforts in order to resolve or mitigate any potential interference problem with the Arecibo Observatory. If the Commission determines that an operator has satisfied its responsibility to make reasonable efforts to protect the Observatory from interference, the unit may be allowed to operate.

[61 FR 46569, Sept. 4, 1996, as amended at 62 FR 55536, Oct. 27, 1997; 70 CFR 31374, June 1, 2005]

§95.1005 Station identification.

An LPRS station is not required to transmit a station identification announcement.

§95.1007 Station inspection.

All LPRS system apparatus must be made available for inspection upon request by an authorized FCC representative.

§95.1009 Permissible communications.

LPRS stations may transmit voice, data, or tracking signals as permitted in this section. Two-way voice communications are prohibited.

(a) Auditory assistance communications (including but not limited to applications such as assistive listening devices, audio description for the blind, and simultaneous language translation) for:

(1) Persons with disabilities. In the context of the LPRS, the term "disability" has the meaning given to it by section 3(2)(A) of the Americans with Disabilities Act of 1990 (42 U.S.C. 12102(2)(A)), *i.e,* persons with a physical or mental impairment

that substantially limits one or more of the major life activities of such individuals;

(2) Persons who require language translation; or

(3) Persons who may otherwise benefit from auditory assistance communications in educational settings.

(b) Health care related communications for the ill.

(c) Law enforcement tracking signals (for homing or interrogation) including the tracking of persons or stolen goods under authority or agreement with a law enforcement agency (federal, state, or local) having jurisdiction in the area where the transmitters are placed.

(d) AMTS point-to-point network control communications.

§95.1011 Channel use policy.

(a) The channels authorized to LPRS systems by this part are available on a shared basis only and will not be assigned for the exclusive use of any entity.

(b) Those using LPRS transmitters must cooperate in the selection and use of channels in order to reduce interference and make the most effective use of the authorized facilities. Channels must be selected in an effort to avoid interference to other LPRS transmissions.

(c) Operation is subject to the conditions that no harmful interference is caused to the United States Navy's SPASUR radar system (216.88-217.08 MHz) or to TV reception within the Grade B contour of any TV channel 13 station or within the 68 dBu predicted contour of any low power TV or TV translator station operating on channel 13.

§95.1013 Antennas.

(a) The maximum allowable ERP for a station in the LPRS other than an AMTS station is 100 mW. The maximum allowable ERP for an AMTS station in the LPRS is 1 W, so long as emissions are attenuated, in accordance with §80.211 of this chapter, at the band edges.

(b) AMTS stations must employ directional antennas.

(c) Antennas used with LPRS units must comply with the following:

(1) For LPRS units operating entirely within an enclosed structure, e.g., a building, there is no limit on antenna height;

(2) For LPRS units not operating entirely within an enclosed structure, the tip of the antenna shall not exceed 30.5 meters (100 feet) above ground. In cases where harmful interference occurs the FCC may require that the antenna height be reduced; and

(3) The height limitation in paragraph (c)(2) of this section does not apply to LPRS units in which the antenna is an integral part of the unit.

[61 FR 46569, Sept. 4, 1996, as amended at 65 FR 77827, Dec. 13, 2000]

§95.1015 Disclosure policies.

(a) Manufacturers of LPRS transmitters used for auditory assistance, health care assistance, and law enforcement tracking purposes must include with each transmitting device the following statement: "This transmitter is authorized by rule under the Low Power Radio Service (47 CFR part 95) and must not cause harmful interference to TV reception or United States Navy SPASUR installations. You do not need an FCC license to operate this transmitter. This transmitter may only be used to provide: auditory assistance to persons with disabilities, persons who require language translation, or persons in educational settings; health care services to the ill; law enforcement tracking services under agreement with a law enforcement agency; or automated maritime telecommunications system (AMTS) network control communications. Two-way voice communications and all other types of uses not mentioned above are expressly prohibited."

(b) Prior to operating a LPRS transmitter for AMTS purposes, an AMTS licensee must notify, in writing, each television station that may be affected by such operations, as defined in §80.215(h) of this chapter. The notification provided with the station's license application is sufficient to satisfy this requirement if no new television stations would be affected.

§95.1017 Labeling requirements.

(a) Each LPRS transmitting device shall bear the following statement in a conspicuous location on the device: "This device may not interfere with TV reception or Federal Government radar."

(b) Where an LPRS device is constructed in two or more sections connected by wires and marketed together, the statement specified in this section is required to be affixed only to the main control unit.

(c) When the LPRS device is so small or for such use that it is not practicable to place the statement specified in the section on it, the statement must be placed in a prominent location in the instruction manual or pamphlet supplied to the user or, alternatively, shall be placed on the container in which the device is marketed.

[61 FR 46569, Sept. 4, 1996, as amended at 67 FR 6193, Feb. 11, 2002]

§95.1019 Marketing limitations.

Transmitters intended for operation in the LPRS may be marketed and sold only for those uses described in §95.1009.

[64 FR 69933, Dec. 15, 1999]

Subpart H—Wireless Medical Telemetry Service (WMTS)

SOURCE: 65 FR 44008, July 17, 2000, unless otherwise noted.

GENERAL PROVISIONS

§95.1101 Scope.

This subpart sets out the regulations governing the operation of Wireless Medical Telemetry Devices in the 608-614 MHz, 1395-1400 MHz, and 1427-1432 MHz frequency bands. *See* §95.630 regarding permissible frequencies.

[75 FR 19285, Apr. 14, 2010]

§95.1103 Definitions.

(a) *Authorized health care provider.* A physician or other individual authorized under state or federal law to provide health care services, or any other health care facility operated by or employing individuals authorized under state or federal law to provide health care services, or any trained technician operating under the supervision and control of an individual or health care facility authorized under state or federal law to provide health care services.

(b) *Health care facility.* A health care facility includes hospitals and other establishments that offer services, facilities and beds for use beyond a 24 hour period in rendering medical treatment, and institutions and organizations regularly engaged in providing medical services through clinics, public health facilities, and similar establishments, including government entities and agencies such as Veterans Administration hospitals; except the term health care facility does not include an ambulance or other moving vehicle.

(c) *Wireless medical telemetry.* The measurement and recording of physiological parameters and other patient-related information via radiated bi-or unidirectional electromagnetic

151

signals in the 608-614, 1395-1400 MHz and 1427-1432 MHz frequency bands.

[65 FR 44008, July 17, 2000, as amended at 67 FR 6194, Feb. 11, 2002; 75 FR 19285, Apr. 14, 2010]

§95.1105 Eligibility.

Authorized health care providers are authorized by rule to operate transmitters in the Wireless Medical Telemetry Service without an individual license issued by the Commission provided the coordination requirements in §95.1111 have been met. Manufacturers of wireless medical telemetry devices and their representatives are authorized to operated wireless medical telemetry transmitters in this service solely for the purpose of demonstrating such equipment to, or installing and maintaining such equipment for, duly authorized health care providers. No entity that is a foreign government or which is active in the capacity as a representative of a foreign government is eligible to operate a WMTS transmitter.

§95.1107 Authorized locations.

The operation of a wireless medical telemetry transmitter under this part is authorized anywhere within a health care facility provided the facility is located anywhere a CB station operation is permitted under §95.405. This authority does not extend to mobile vehicles, such as ambulances, even if those vehicles are associated with a health care facility.

§95.1109 Equipment authorization requirement.

(a) Wireless medical telemetry devices operating under this part must be authorized under the certification procedure prior to marketing or use in accordance with the provisions of part 2, subpart J of this chapter.

(b) Each device shall be labeled with the following statement:

Operation of this equipment requires the prior coordination with a frequency coordinator designated by the FCC for the Wireless Medical Telemetry Service.

§95.1111 Frequency coordination.

(a) Prior to operation, authorized health care providers who desire to use wireless medical telemetry devices must register all devices with a designated frequency coordinator. Except as specified in §95.1105, operation of WMTS equipment prior to registration is not authorized under this part. The registration must include the following information:

(1) Specific frequencies or frequency range(s) used;

(2) Modulation scheme used (including occupied bandwidth);

(3) Effective radiated power;

(4) Number of transmitters in use at the health care facility as of the date of registration including manufacturer name(s) and model numbers);

(5) Legal name of the authorized health care provider;

(6) Location of transmitter (coordinates, street address, building);

(7) Point of contact for the authorized health care provider (name, title, office, phone number, fax number, e-mail address).

(b) An authorized health care provider shall notify the frequency coordinator whenever a medical telemetry device is permanently taken out of service, unless the device is replaced with another transmitter utilizing the same technical characteristics as those reported on the effective registration. An authorized health care provider shall maintain the information contained in each registration current in all material respects, and shall notify the frequency coordinator when any change is made in the location or operating parameters previously reported which is material.

(c) As of April 14, 2010, no registrations may be accepted for frequencies where WMTS does not have primary status. Previously registered secondary facilities may continue to operate as registered.

[65 FR 44008, July 17, 2000, as amended at 75 FR 19285, Apr. 14, 2010]

§95.1113 Frequency coordinator.

(a) The Commission will designate a frequency coordinator(s) to manage the usage of the frequency bands for the operation of medical telemetry devices.

(b) The frequency coordinator shall

(1) Review and process coordination requests submitted by authorized health care providers as required in §95.1111;

(2) Maintain a database of WMTS use;

(3) Notify users of potential conflicts; and

(4) Coordinate WMTS operation with radio astronomy observatories and Federal Government radar systems as specified in §§95.1119 and 95.1121.

(5) Notify licensees—who are operating in accordance with §90.259(b)—of the need to comply with the field strength limit of §90.259(b)(11) prior to initial activation of WMTS equipment in the 1427-1432 MHz band.

(6) Notify licensees—who are operating in 1392-1395 MHz band in accordance with subpart I of part 27—of the need to comply with the field strength limit of §27.804 prior to initial activation of WMTS equipment in the 1395-1400 MHz band.

[65 FR 44008, July 17, 2000, as amended at 67 FR 41682, June 20, 2002]

§95.1115 General technical requirements.

(a) *Field strength limits.* (1) In the 608-614 MHz band, the maximum allowable field strength is 200 mV/m, as measured at a distance of 3 meters, using measuring instrumentation with a CISPR quasi-peak detector.

(2) In the 1395-1400 MHz and 1427-1432 MHz bands, the maximum allowable field strength is 740 mV/m, as measured at a distance of 3 meters, using measuring equipment with an averaging detector and a 1MHz measurement bandwidth.

(b) *Undesired emissions.* (1) Out-of-band emissions below 960 MHz are limited to 200 microvolts/meter, as measured at a distance of 3 meters, using measuring instrumentation with a CISPR quasi-peak detector.

(2) Out-of-band emissions above 960 MHz are limited to 500 microvolts/meter as measured at a distance of 3 meters, using measuring equipment with an averaging detector and a 1 MHz measurement bandwidth.

(c) *Emission types.* A wireless medical telemetry device may transmit any emission type appropriate for communications in this service, except for video and voice. Waveforms such as electrocardiograms (ECGs) are not considered video.

(d) *Channel use.* (1) In the 1395-1400 MHz and 1427-1432 MHz bands, no specific channels are specified. Wireless medical telemetry devices may operate on any channel within the bands authorized for wireless medical telemetry use in this part.

(2) In the 608-614 MHz band, wireless medical telemetry devices utilizing broadband technologies such as spread spectrum shall be capable of operating within one or more of the following channels of 1.5 MHz each, up to a maximum of 6 MHz, and shall operate on the minimum number of channels

necessary to avoid harmful interference to any other wireless medical telemetry devices.

608.0-609.5 MHz

609.5-611.0 MHz

611.0-612.5 MHz

612.5-614.0 MHz

(3) Channel usage is on a co-primary shared basis only, and channels will not be assigned for the exclusive use of any entity.

(4) Authorized health care providers, in conjunction with the equipment manufacturers, must cooperate in the selection and use of frequencies in order to reduce the potential for interference with other wireless medical telemetry devices, or other co-primary users. Operations in the 608-614 MHz band (television channel 37) are not protected from adjacent band interference from broadcast television operating on channels 36 and 38.

(e) *Frequency stability.* Manufacturers of wireless medical telemetry devices are responsible for ensuring frequency stability such that an emission is maintained within the band of operation under all of the manufacturer's specified conditions.

[65 FR 44008, July 17, 2000, as amended at 67 FR 6194, Feb. 11, 2002; 68 FR 68547, Dec. 9, 2003; 75 FR 19285, Apr. 14, 2010]

§95.1117 Types of communications.

(a) All types of communications except voice and video are permitted, on both a unidirectional and bidirectional basis, provided that all such communications are related to the provision of medical care. Waveforms such as electrocardiograms (ECGs) are not considered video.

(b) Operations that comply with the requirements of this part may be conducted under manual or automatic control, and on a continuous basis.

§95.1119 Specific requirements for wireless medical telemetry devices operating in the 608-614 MHz band.

For a wireless medical telemetry device operating within the frequency range 608-614 MHz and that will be located near the radio astronomy observatories listed below, operation is not permitted until a WMTS frequency coordinator specified in §95.1113 has coordinated with, and obtain the written concurrence of, the director of the affected radio astronomy observatory before the equipment can be installed or operated

(a) Within 80 kilometers of:

(1) National Astronomy and Ionosphere Center, Arecibo, Puerto Rico: 18°20′38.28″ North Latitude, 66°45′09.42″ West Longitude.

(2) National Radio Astronomy Observatory, Socorro, New Mexico: 34°04′43″ North Latitude, 107°37′04″ West Longitude.

(3) National Radio Astronomy Observatory, Green Bank, West Virginia: 38°26′08″ North Latitude, 79°49′42″ West Longitude.

(b) Within 32 kilometers of the National Radio Astronomy Observatory centered on:

Very long baseline array stations	Latitude (North)	Longitude (West)
Pie Town, NM	34°18'	108°07'
Kitt Peak, AZ	31°57'	111°37'
Los Alamos, NM	35°47'	106°15'
Fort Davis, TX	30°38'	103°57'
North Liberty, IA	41°46'	91°34'
Brewster, WA	48°08'	119°41'
Owens Valley, CA	37°14'	118°17'
Saint Croix, VI	17°46'	64°35'
Mauna Kea, HI	19°49'	155°28'
Hancock, NH	42°56'	71°59'

The National Science Foundation point of contact for coordination is: Spectrum Manager, Division of Astronomical Sciences, NSF Room 1045, 4201 Wilson Blvd., Arlington, VA 22230, telephone: 703-306-1823.

§95.1121 Specific requirements for wireless medical telemetry devices operating in the 1395-1400 and 1427-1432 MHz bands.

Due to the critical nature of communications transmitted under this part, the frequency coordinator in consultation with the National Telecommunications and Information Administration shall determine whether there are any Federal Government systems whose operations could affect, or could be affected by,

158

proposed wireless medical telemetry operations in the 1395-1400 MHz and 1427-1432 MHz bands. The locations of government systems in these bands are specified in footnotes US351 and US352 of §2.106 of this chapter.

[75 FR 19285, Apr. 14, 2010]

§95.1123 Protection of medical equipment.

The manufacturers, installers and users of WMTS equipment are cautioned that the operation of this equipment could result in harmful interference to other nearby medical devices.

§95.1125 RF safety.

Portable devices as defined in §2.1093(b) of this chapter operating in the WMTS are subject to radio frequency radiation exposure requirements as specified in §§1.1307(b) and 2.1093 of this chapter. Applications for equipment authorization of WMTS devices must contain a statement confirming compliance with these requirements. Technical information showing the basis for this statement must be submitted to the Commission upon request.

§95.1127 Station identification.

A WMTS station is not required to transmit a station identification announcement.

§95.1129 Station inspection.

All WMTS transmitters must be available for inspection upon request by an authorized FCC representative.

Subpart I—Medical Device Radiocommunication Service (MedRadio)

SOURCE: 74 FR 22709, May 14, 2009, unless otherwise noted.

§95.1201 Eligibility.

Operation in the MedRadio service is permitted by rule and without an individual license issued by the FCC. Duly authorized health care professionals are permitted to operate MedRadio transmitters. Persons may also operate MedRadio transmitters to the extent the transmitters are incorporated into implanted or body-worn medical devices that are used by the person at the direction of a duly authorized health care professional; this includes medical devices that have been implanted in that person or placed on the body of that person by or under the direction of a duly authorized health care professional. Manufacturers of medical devices that include MedRadio transmitters, and their representatives, are authorized to operate transmitters in this service for the purpose of demonstrating such equipment to duly authorized health care professionals. No entity that is a foreign government or which is acting in its capacity as a representative of a foreign government is eligible to operate a MedRadio transmitter. The term "duly authorized health care professional" means a physician or other individual authorized under state or federal law to provide health care services. Operations that comply with the requirements of this part may be conducted under manual or automatic control.

§95.1203 Authorized locations.

MedRadio operation is authorized anywhere CB station operation is authorized under §95.405, except that use of Medical Body Area Network devices in the 2360-2390 MHz band is restricted to indoor operation within a health care facility registered with the MBAN coordinator under §95.1225. A health care facility includes hospitals and other establishments that offer services, facilities and beds for use beyond a 24 hour period in rendering medical treatment, and institutions and organizations regularly engaged in providing medical services through clinics, public health facilities, and similar

160

establishments, including government entities and agencies such as Veterans Administration hospitals

[77 FR 55732, Sept. 11, 2012]

§95.1205 Station identification.

A station is not required to transmit a station identification announcement.

§95.1207 Station inspection.

Any non-implanted MedRadio transmitter must be made available for inspection upon request by an authorized FCC representative. Persons operating implanted or body-worn MedRadio transmitters shall cooperate reasonably with duly authorized FCC representatives in the resolution of interference.

§95.1209 Permissible communications.

(a) Except for the purposes of testing and for demonstrations to health care professionals, MedRadio programmer/control transmitters may transmit only non-voice data containing operational, diagnostic and therapeutic information associated with a medical implant device or medical body-worn device that has been implanted or placed on the person by or under the direction of a duly authorized health care professional.

(b) Except as provided in §95.627(b) no MedRadio implant or body-worn transmitter shall transmit except in response to a transmission from a MedRadio programmer/control transmitter or in response to a non-radio frequency actuation signal generated by a device external to the body with respect to which the MedRadio implant or body-worn transmitter is used.

(c) MedRadio programmer/control transmitters may be interconnected with other telecommunications systems including the public switched telephone network.

(d) For the purpose of facilitating MedRadio system operation during a MedRadio communications session, as defined in §95.627, MedRadio transmitters in the 401-406 MHz band may transmit in accordance with the provisions of §95.627(a) for no more than 5 seconds without the communications of data; MedRadio transmitters may transmit in accordance with the provisions of §95.627(b)(2) and (b)(3) for no more than 3.6 seconds in total within a one hour time period; and MedRadio transmitters may transmit in accordance with the provisions of §95.627(b)(4) for no more than 360 milliseconds in total within a one hour time period.

(e) MedRadio programmer/control transmitters may not be used to relay information in the 401-406 MHz band to a receiver that is not included with a medical implant or medical body-worn device. Wireless retransmission of information intended to be transmitted by a MedRadio programmer/control transmitter or information received from a medical implant or medical body-worn transmitter shall be performed using other radio services that operate in spectrum outside of the 401-406 MHz band.

(f) MedRadio programmer/control transmitters and medical implant transmitters may not be used to relay information in the 413-419 MHz, 426-432 MHz, 438-444 MHz, and 451-457 MHz bands to a receiver that is not part of the same Medical Micropower Network. Wireless retransmission of information to a receiver that is not part of the same Medical Micropower Network must be performed using other radio services that operate in spectrum outside of the 413-419 MHz, 426-432 MHz, 438-444 MHz, and 451-457 MHz bands. Not withstanding the above restrictions, a MedRadio programmer/control transmitter of an MMN may communicate with the MedRadio programmer/control transmitter of another MMN to coordinate transmissions so as to avoid interference between the two MMNs.

(g) Medical body-worn transmitters may only relay information in the 2360-2400 MHz band to a MedRadio programmer/control transmitter that is part of the same Medical Body Area Network (MBAN). A MedRadio programmer/control transmitter may not be used to relay information in the 2360-2400 MHz band to another MedRadio programmer/controller transmitter. Wireless retransmission of information to a receiver that is not part of the same MBAN shall be performed using other radio services that operate in spectrum outside of the 2360-2400 MHz band.

(h) MedRadio programmer/control transmitters operating in the 413-419 MHz, 426-432 MHz, 438-444 MHz, and 451-457 MHz bands shall not transmit with a duty cycle greater than 3 percent.

[74 FR 22709, May 14, 2009, as amended at 75 FR 52477, Aug. 26, 2010; 77 FR 4269, Jan. 27, 2012; 77 FR 55733, Sept. 11, 2012]

§95.1211 Channel use policy.

(a) The channels authorized for MedRadio operation by this part of the FCC Rules are available on a shared basis only and will not be assigned for the exclusive use of any entity.

(b) To reduce interference and make the most effective use of the authorized facilities, MedRadio transmitters must share the spectrum in accordance with §§95.627 or 95.628.

(c) MedRadio operation is subject to the condition that no harmful interference is caused to stations operating in the 400.150-406.000 MHz band in the Meteorological Aids, Meteorological Satellite, or Earth Exploration Satellite Services, or to other authorized stations operating in the 413-419 MHz, 426-432 MHz, 438-444 MHz, 451-457, and 2360-2400 MHz bands. MedRadio stations must accept any interference from stations operating in the 400.150-406.000 MHz band in the Meteorological Aids, Meteorological Satellite, or Earth Exploration Satellite Services, and from other authorized stations operating in the 413-419 MHz, 426-432 MHz, 438-444 MHz, 451-457, and 2360-2400 MHz bands.

[74 FR 22709, May 14, 2009, as amended at 77 FR 4270, Jan. 27, 2012; 77 FR 55733, Sept. 11, 2012]

§95.1213 Antennas.

Except for the 2390-2400 MHz band, no antenna for a MedRadio transmitter shall be configured for permanent outdoor use. In addition, any MedRadio antenna used outdoors shall not be affixed to any structure for which the height to the tip of the antenna will exceed three (3) meters (9.8 feet) above ground.

[77 FR 55733, Sept. 11, 2012

§95.1215 Disclosure policies.

(a) Manufacturers of MedRadio transmitters operating in the 401-406 MHz band must include with each transmitting device the following statement:

"This transmitter is authorized by rule under the Medical Device Radio communication Service (in part 95 of the FCC Rules) and must not cause harmful interference to stations operating in the 400.150-406.000 MHz band in the Meteorological Aids (*i.e.,* transmitters and receivers used to communicate weather data), the Meteorological Satellite, or the Earth Exploration Satellite Services and must accept interference that may be caused by such stations, including interference that may cause undesired operation. This transmitter shall be used only in accordance with the FCC Rules governing the Medical Device Radio communication Service. Analog and digital voice communications are prohibited. Although this transmitter has been approved by the Federal Communications Commission, there is no guarantee that it will not receive interference or that any particular transmission from this transmitter will be free from interference."

(b) Manufacturers of MedRadio transmitters operating in the 413-419 MHz, 426-432 MHz, 438-444 MHz, and 451-457 MHz bands must include with each transmitting device the following statement:

"This transmitter is authorized by rule under the MedRadio Service (47 CFR part 95). This transmitter must not cause harmful interference to stations authorized to operate on a primary basis in the 413-419 MHz, 426-432 MHz, 438-444 MHz, and 451-457 MHz bands, and must accept interference that may be caused by such stations, including interference that may cause undesired operation. This transmitter shall be used only in accordance with the FCC Rules governing the MedRadio Service. Analog and digital voice

164

communications are prohibited. Although this transmitter has been approved by the Federal Communications Commission, there is no guarantee that it will not receive interference or that any particular transmission from this transmitter will be free from interference."

(c) Manufacturers of MedRadio transmitters operating in the 2360-2400 MHz band must include with each transmitting device the following statement:

"This transmitter is authorized by rule under the MedRadio Service (47 CFR part 95). This transmitter must not cause harmful interference to stations authorized to operate on a primary basis in the 2360-2400 MHz band, and must accept interference that may be caused by such stations, including interference that may cause undesired operation. This transmitter shall be used only in accordance with the FCC Rules governing the MedRadio Service. Analog and digital voice communications are prohibited. Although this transmitter has been approved by the Federal Communications Commission, there is no guarantee that it will not receive interference or that any particular transmission from this transmitter will be free from interference."

[77 FR 4270, Jan. 27, 2012, as amended at 77 FR 55733, Sept. 11, 2012]

§95.1217 Labeling requirements.

(a)(1) MedRadio programmer/control transmitters operating in the 401-406 MHz band shall be labeled as provided in part 2 of this chapter and shall bear the following statement in a conspicuous location on the device:

"This device may not interfere with stations operating in the 400.150-406.000 MHz band in the Meteorological Aids, Meteorological Satellite, and Earth Exploration Satellite Services and must accept any interference received, including interference that may cause undesired operation."

The statement may be placed in the instruction manual for the transmitter where it is not feasible to place the statement on the device.

(2) MedRadio programmer/control transmitters operating in the 413-419 MHz, 426-432 MHz, 438-444 MHz, and 451-457 MHz bands shall be labeled as provided in part 2 of this chapter and shall bear the following statement in a conspicuous location on the device:

"This device may not interfere with stations authorized to operate on a primary basis in the 413-419 MHz, 426-432 MHz, 438-444 MHz, and 451-457 MHz bands, and must accept any interference received, including interference that may cause undesired operation."

The statement may be placed in the instruction manual for the transmitter where it is not feasible to place the statement on the device.

(3) MedRadio programmer/control transmitters operating in the 2360-2400 MHz band shall be labeled as provided in part 2 of this chapter and shall bear the following statement in a conspicuous location on the device:

"This device may not interfere with stations authorized to operate on a primary basis in the 2360-2400 MHz band, and must accept any interference received, including interference that may cause undesired operation."

The statement may be placed in the instruction manual for the transmitter where it is not feasible to place the statement on the device.

(b) Where a MedRadio programmer/control transmitter is constructed in two or more sections connected by wire and marketed together, the statement specified in this section is required to be affixed only to the main control unit.

(c) MedRadio transmitters shall be identified with a serial number, except that in the 2360-2400 MHz band only the MedRadio programmer/controller transmitter shall be identified with a serial number. The FCC ID number associated with a medical implant transmitter and the information required by §2.925 of this chapter may be placed in the instruction manual for the transmitter and on the shipping container for the transmitter, in lieu of being placed directly on the transmitter.

[74 FR 22709, May 14, 2009, as amended at 77 FR 4270, Jan. 27, 2012; 77 FR 55734, Sept. 11, 2012]

§95.1219 Marketing limitations.

Transmitters intended for operation in the MedRadio Service may be marketed and sold only for the permissible communications described in §95.1209.

§95.1221 RF exposure.

A MedRadio medical implant device or medical body-worn transmitter is subject to the radiofrequency radiation exposure requirements specified in §§1.1307(b) and 2.1093 of this chapter, as appropriate. Applications for equipment authorization of devices operating under this section must demonstrate compliance with these requirements using either finite difference time domain (FDTD) computational modeling or laboratory measurement techniques. Where a showing is based on computational modeling, the Commission retains the discretion to request that supporting documentation and/or specific absorption rate (SAR) measurement data be submitted.

[78 FR 33653, June 4, 2013]

§95.1223 Registration and frequency coordination in the 2360-2390 MHz Band.

(a) *Registration.* A health care facility must register all MBAN devices it proposes to operate in the 2360-2390 MHz band with a frequency coordinator designated under §95.1225 of this chapter. Operation of these devices in the 2360-2390 MHz band is prohibited prior to the MBAN coordinator notifying the health care facility that registration and coordination (to the extent coordination is required under paragraph (c) of this section), is complete. The registration must include the following information:

(1) Specific frequencies or frequency range(s) within the 2360-2390 MHz band to be used, and the capabilities of the MBAN equipment to use the 2390-2400 MHz band;

(2) Effective isotropic radiated power;

(3) Number of control transmitters in use at the health care facility as of the date of registration including manufacturer name(s) and model numbers and FCC identification number;

(4) Legal name of the health care facility;

(5) Location of control transmitters (*e.g.*, geographic coordinates, street address, building);

(6) Point of contact for the health care facility (*e.g.*, name, title, office, phone number, fax number, email address); and

(7) In the event an MBAN has to cease operating in all or a portion of the 2360-2390 MHz band due to interference under §95.1211 or changes in coordination under paragraph (c) of this section, a point of contact (including contractors) for the health care facility that is responsible for ensuring that this change is effected whenever it is required (*e.g.*, name, title, office, phone number, fax number, email address). The health care facility also must state whether, in such cases, its MBAN operation is capable of defaulting to the 2390-2400 MHz band and that it is responsible for ceasing MBAN operations in the 2360-2390 MHz band or defaulting traffic to other hospital systems.

(b) *Notification.* A health care facility shall notify the frequency coordinator whenever an MBAN control transmitter in the 2360-2390 MHz band is permanently taken out of service, unless it is replaced with transmitter(s) using the same technical characteristics as those reported on the health care facility's registration. A health care facility shall keep the information contained in each registration current, shall notify the frequency coordinator of any material change to the MBAN's location or operating parameters, and is prohibited from operating the MBAN in the 2360-2390 MHz band under changed operating parameters until the frequency coordinator determines whether such changes require coordination with the AMT coordinator designated under §87.305 of this chapter and, if so, the coordination required under paragraph (c) of this section has been completed.

(c) *Coordination procedures.* The frequency coordinator will determine if an MBAN is within the line of sight of an AMT receive facility in the 2360-2390 MHz band and notify the health care facility when it may begin MBAN operations under the applicable procedures in (c)(1) or (2) of this section.

(1) If the MBAN is beyond the line of sight of an AMT receive facility, it may operate without prior coordination with the AMT coordinator, provided that the MBAN coordinator provides the AMT coordinator with the MBAN registration information and the AMT coordinator concurs that the MBAN is beyond the line of sight prior to the MBAN beginning operations in the band.

(2) If the MBAN is within line of sight of an AMT receive facility, the MBAN frequency coordinator shall achieve a mutually satisfactory coordination agreement with the AMT frequency coordinator prior to the MBAN beginning operations in the band. Such coordination agreement shall provide protection to AMT receive stations consistent with International Telecommunication Union (ITU) Recommendation ITU-R M.1459, "Protection criteria for telemetry systems in the aeronautical mobile service and mitigation techniques to facilitate sharing with geostationary broadcasting-satellite and mobile-satellite services in the frequency bands 1 452-1 525 and 2 310-2 360 MHz," May 2000, as adjusted using generally accepted engineering practices and standards that are mutually agreeable to both coordinators to take into account the local conditions and operating characteristics of the applicable AMT and MBAN facilities, and shall specify when the device shall limit its transmissions to segments of the 2360-2390 MHz band or shall cease operation in the band. This ITU document is incorporated by reference in accordance with 5 U.S.C. 552(a) and 1 CFR part 51 and approved by the Director of Federal Register. Copies of the recommendation may be obtained from ITU, Place des Nations, 1211 Geneva 20, Switzerland, or online at *http://www.itu.int/en/publications/Pages/default.aspx*. You may inspect a copy at the Federal Communications Commission, 445

12th Street, SW., Washington, DC 20554, or at the National Archives and Records Administration (NARA). For information on the availability of this material at NARA, call 202-741-6030, or go to: *http://www.archives.gov/federal_register/code_of_federal_regula tions/ibr_locations.html.* "Generally accepted engineering practices and standards" include, but are not limited to, engineering analyses and measurement data as well as limiting MBAN operations in the band by time or frequency.

(3) If an AMT operator plans to operate a receive site not previously analyzed by the MBAN coordinator to determine line of sight to an MBAN facility, the AMT operator shall consider using locations that are beyond the line of sight of a registered health care facility. If the AMT operator determines that non-line of sight locations are not practical for its purposes, the AMT coordinator shall notify the MBAN coordinator upon no less than 7 days' notice that the registered health care facility must cease MBAN operations in the 2360-2390 MHz band unless the parties can achieve a mutually satisfactory coordination agreement under paragraph (c)(2) of this section.

[77 FR 55734, Sept. 11, 2012]

§95.1225 Frequency coordinator.

(a) The Commission will designate a frequency coordinator(s) to manage the operation of medical body area networks in the 2360 MHz -2390 MHz band.

(b) The frequency coordinator shall perform the following functions:

(1) Register health care facilities that operate an MBAN in the 2360-2390 MHz band, maintain a database of these MBAN transmitter locations and operational parameters, and provide the Commission with information contained in the database upon request;

(2) Determine if an MBAN is within line of sight of an AMT receive facility in the 2360-2390 MHz band and coordinate

170

MBAN operations with the designated AMT coordinator as specified in §87.305 of this chapter;

(3) Notify a registered health care facility when an MBAN has to change frequency within the 2360-2390 MHz band or to cease operating in the band consistent with a coordination agreement between the MBAN and the AMT coordinators;

(4) Develop procedures to ensure that registered health care facilities operate an MBAN consistent with the coordination requirements under §95.1223; and

(5) Identify the MBAN that is the source of interference in response to a complaint from the AMT coordinator and notify the health care facility of alternative frequencies available for MBAN use or to cease operation consistent with the rules.

[77 FR 55735, Sept. 11, 2012]

Subpart J—Multi-Use Radio Service (MURS)

SOURCE: 65 FR 60878, Oct. 13, 2000, unless otherwise noted.

GENERAL PROVISIONS

§95.1301 Eligibility.

An entity is authorized by rule to operate a MURS transmitter if it is not a foreign government or a representative of a foreign government and if it uses the transmitter in accordance with §95.1309 and otherwise operates in accordance with the rules contained in this subpart. No license will be issued.

§95.1303 Authorized locations.

(a) MURS operation is authorized:

(1) Anywhere CB station operation is permitted under §95.405; and

(2) Aboard any vessel of the United States, with the permission of the captain, while the vessel is travelling either domestically or in international waters.

(b) MURS operation is not authorized aboard aircraft in flight.

(c) Anyone intending to operate a MURS unit on the islands of Puerto Rico, Desecheo, Mona, Vieques, and Culebra in a manner that could pose an interference threat to the Arecibo Observatory shall notify the Interference Office, Arecibo Observatory, HC3 Box 53995, Arecibo, Puerto Rico 00612, in writing or electronically, of the location of the unit. Operators may wish to consult interference guidelines, which will be provided by Cornell University. Operators who choose to transmit information electronically should e-mail to: *prcz@naic.edu.*

(1) The notification to the Interference Office, Arecibo Observatory shall be made 45 days prior to commencing

operation of the unit. The notification shall state the geographical coordinates of the unit.

(2) After receipt of such notifications, the Commission will allow the Arecibo Observatory a period of 20 days for comments or objections. The operator will be required to make reasonable efforts in order to resolve or mitigate any potential interference problem with the Arecibo Observatory. If the Commission determines that an operator has satisfied its responsibility to make reasonable efforts to protect the Observatory from interference, the unit may be allowed to operate.

[65 FR 60878, Oct. 13, 2000, as amended at 70 FR 31374, June 1, 2005]

§95.1305 Station identification.

A MURS station is not required to transmit a station identification announcement.

§95.1307 Permissible communications.

(a) MURS stations may transmit voice or data signals as permitted in this subpart.

(b) A MURS station may transmit any emission type listed in §95.631(j) of this chapter.

(c) MURS frequencies may be used for remote control and telemetering functions. MURS transmitters may not be operated in the continuous carrier transmit mode.

(d) MURS users shall take reasonable precautions to avoid causing harmful interference. This includes monitoring the transmitting frequency for communications in progress and such other measures as may be necessary to minimize the potential for causing interference.

[67 FR 63290, Oct. 11, 2002]

§95.1309 Channel use policy.

(a) The channels authorized to MURS systems by this part are available on a shared basis only and will not be assigned for the exclusive use of any entity.

(b) Those using MURS transmitters must cooperate in the selection and use of channels in order to reduce interference and make the most effective use of authorized facilities. Channels must be selected in an effort to avoid interference to other MURS transmissions.

§95.1311 Repeater operations and signal boosters prohibited.

MURS stations are prohibited from operating as a repeater station or as a signal booster. This prohibition includes store-and-forward packet operation.

[67 FR 63290, Oct. 11, 2002]

§95.1313 Interconnection prohibited.

MURS stations are prohibited from interconnection with the public switched network. *Interconnection Defined.* Connection through automatic or manual means of multi-use radio stations with the facilities of the public switched telephone network to permit the transmission of messages or signals between points in the wireline or radio network of a public telephone company and persons served by multi-use radio stations. Wireline or radio circuits or links furnished by common carriers, which are used by licensees or other authorized persons for transmitter control (including dial-up transmitter control circuits) or as an integral part of an authorized, private, internal system of communication or as an integral part of dispatch point circuits in a multi-use radio station are not considered to be interconnection for purposes of this rule part.

[67 FR 63290, Oct. 11, 2002]

§95.1315 Antenna height restriction.

The highest point of any MURS antenna must no be more than 18.3 meters (60 feet) above the ground or 6.10 meters (20 feet) above the highest point of the structure on which it is mounted.

[67 FR 63290, Oct. 11, 2002]

§95.1317 Grandfathered MURS Stations.

Stations that were licensed under part 90 of the Commission's Rules to operate on MURS frequencies as of November 13, 2000, are granted a license by rule that authorizes continued operations under the terms of such nullified part 90 authorizations, including any rule waivers.

[67 FR 63290, Oct. 11, 2002]

Subpart K—Personal Locator Beacons (PLB)

SOURCE: 68 FR 32678, June 2, 2003, unless otherwise noted.

§95.1400 Basis and purpose.

The rules in this subpart are intended to provide individuals in remote areas a means to alert others of an emergency situation and to aid search and rescue personnel locate those in distress. The effective date for the rules in this subpart will be July 1, 2003.

§95.1401 Frequency.

The frequency band 406.0-406.1 MHz is an emergency and distress frequency band available for use by Personal Locator Beacons (PLBs). Personal Locator Beacons that transmit on the frequency band 406.0-406.1 MHz must use G1D emission. Use of these frequencies must be limited to transmission of distress and safety communications.

§95.1402 Special requirements for 406 MHz PLBs.

(a) All 406 MHz PLBs must meet all the technical and performance standards contained in the Radio Technical Commission for Maritime (RTCM) Service document "RTCM Recommended Standards for 406 MHz Satellite Personal Locator Beacons (PLBs)," Version 1.1, RTCM Paper 76-2002/SC110-STD, dated June 19, 2002. This RTCM document is incorporated by reference in accordance with 5 U.S.C. 552(a), and 1 CFR part 51. Copies of the document are available and may be obtained from the Radio Technical Commission for Maritime Services, 1800 Diagonal Road, Suite 600, Alexandria, Virginia 22314-2840. The document is available for inspection at Commission headquarters at 445 12th Street SW., Washington, DC 20554. Copies may also be inspected at the National Archives and Records Administration (NARA). For information on the availability of this material at NARA, call 202-741-6030, or go to:
http://www.archives.gov/federal_register/code_of_federal_regulations/ibr_locations.html.

(b) The 406 MHz PLB must contain, as an integral part, a homing beacon operating only on 121.500 MHz and meeting all requirements described in the RTCM Recommended Standards document described in paragraph (a) of this section. The 121.500 MHz homing beacon must have a continuous duty cycle that can be interrupted only during the transmission of the 406 MHz signal. The 406 MHz PLB shall transmit a unique identifier (Morse code "P") on the 121.500 MHz signals.

(c) Before a 406 MHz PLB certification application is submitted to the Commission, the applicant must have obtained certification from a test facility, recognized by one of the COSPAS/SARSAT Partners that the PLB satisfies the standards contained in the COSPAS/SARSAT document COSPAS/SARSAT 406 MHz Distress Beacon Type Approval Standard (C/S T.007). Additionally, an independent test facility must certify that the PLB complies with the electrical and environmental standards associated with the RTCM Recommended Standards.

(d) The procedures of Notification by the equipment manufacturer and Certification from either the Commission or designated Telecommunications Certification Body are contained in subpart J of part 2 of this chapter.

(e) An identification code, issued by the National Oceanic and Atmospheric Administration (NOAA), the United States Program Manager for the 406 MHz COSPAS/SARSAT satellite system, must be programmed in each PLB unit to establish a unique identification for each PLB station. With each marketable PLB unit, the manufacturer or grantee must include a postage pre-paid registration card printed with the PLB identification code addressed to: SARSAT Beacon Registration, NOAA, NESDIS, E/SP3, Room 3320, FB-4, 5200 Auth Road, Suitland, Maryland 20746-4303. The registration card must request the owner's name, address, telephone number, alternate emergency contact and include the following statement: "WARNING" failure to register this PLB with NOAA could result in a monetary forfeiture order being issued to the owner."

(f) To enhance protection of life and property, it is mandatory that each 406 MHz PLB be registered with NOAA and that information be kept up-to-date. In addition to the identification plate or label requirements contained in §§2.925 and 2.926 of this chapter, each 406 MHz PLB must be provided on the outside with a clearly discernable permanent plate or label containing the following statement: "The owner of this 406 MHz PLB must register the NOAA identification code contained on this label with the National Oceanic and Atmospheric Administration (NOAA) whose address is: SARSAT Beacon Registration, NOAA, NESDIS, E/SP3, Room 3320, FB-4, 5200 Auth Road, Suitland, Maryland 20746-4303." Owners shall advise NOAA in writing upon change of PLB ownership, or any other change in registration information. NOAA will provide registrants with proof of registration and change of registration postcards.

(g) For 406 MHz PLBs with identification codes that can be changed after manufacture, the identification code shown on the plate or label must be easily replaceable using commonly available tools.

Subpart L—Dedicated Short-Range Communications Service On-Board Units (DSRCS-OBUs)

SOURCE: 69 FR 46446, Aug. 3, 2004, unless otherwise noted.

§95.1501 Scope.

This subpart sets out the regulations governing Dedicated Short-Range Communications Service On-Board Units (DSRCS-OBUs) in the 5850-5925 MHz band. DSRCS Roadside Units (RSUs) are authorized under part 90 of this chapter and DSRCS, RSU, and OBU are defined in §90.7 of this chapter.

§95.1503 Eligibility.

All entities for which the Commission has licensing authority are authorized by rule to operate an FCC certified On-Board Unit in accordance with the rules contained in this subpart. No individual FCC license will be issued. (The FCC does not have authority to license foreign governments or their representatives, nor stations belonging to and operated by the United States Government.)

§95.1505 Authorized locations.

Operation of DSRCS On-Board Units is authorized anywhere CB station operation is permitted under §95.405.

§95.1507 Station Identification.

A DSRCS On-Board Unit is not required to transmit an FCC station identification announcement.

§95.1509 ASTM E2213-03 DSRC Standard.

On-Board Units operating in the 5850-5925 MHz band shall comply with the following technical standards, which are incorporated by reference: American Society for Testing and

Materials (ASTM) E2213-03, Standard Specification for Telecommunications and Information Exchange Between Roadside and Vehicle Systems—5 GHz Band Dedicated Short Range Communications (DSRC) Medium Access Control (MAC) and Physical Layer (PHY) Specifications published September 2003 (ASTM E2213-03 DSRC Standard). The Director of the Federal Register approves this incorporation by reference in accordance with 5 U.S.C. 552(a) and 1 CFR part 51. Copies may be inspected at the Federal Communications Commission, 445 12th Street, SW., Washington, DC 20554 or National Archives and Records Administration (NARA). For information on the availability of this material at NARA, call 202-741-6030, or go to: *http://www.archives.gov/federal_register/code_of_federal_regulations/ibr_locations.html.* Copies of the ASTM E2213-03 DSRC Standard can be obtained from ASTM International, 100 Barr Harbor Drive, PO Box C700, West Conshohocken, PA 19428-2959. Copies may also be obtained from ASTM via the Internet at *http://www.astm.org.*

95.1511 Frequencies available.

(a) The following table indicates the channel designations of frequencies available for assignment to eligible applicants within the 5850-5925 MHz band for On-Board Units (OBUs):[1]

Channel No.	Channel Use	Frequency Range (MHz)
170	Reserved	5850-5855
172	Service Channel[2]	5855-5865
174	Service Channel	5865-5875
175	Service Channel[3]	5865-5885
176	Service Channel	5875-5885
178	Control Channel	5885-5895
180	Service Channel	5895-5905
181	Service Channel[3]	5895-5915
182	Service Channel	5905-5915
184	Service Channel[4]	5915-5925

[1]The maximum output power for portable DSRCS-OBUs is 1.0 mW. *See* §95.639(i).

[2]Channel 172 is designated for public safety applications involving safety of life and property.

[3]Channel Nos. 174/176 may be combined to create a twenty megahertz channel, designated Channel No. 175. Channels 180/182 may be combined to create a twenty-megahertz channel, designated Channel No. 181.

[4]Channel 184 is designated for public safety applications involving safety of life and property.

(b) Except as provided in paragraph (c) of this section, non-reserve DSRCS channels are available on a shared basis only for use in accordance with the Commission's rules. All licensees shall cooperate in the selection and use of channels in order to reduce interference. This includes monitoring for communications in progress and any other measures as may be necessary to minimize interference. Licensees suffering or causing harmful interference within a communications zone are expected to cooperate and resolve this problem by mutually satisfactory arrangements. If the licensees are unable to do so, the Commission may impose restrictions, including specifying the transmitter power, antenna height and direction, additional filtering, or area or hours of operation of the stations concerned. Further, the use of any channel at a given geographical location may be denied when, in the judgment of the Commission, its use at that location is not in the public interest; the use of any channel may be restricted as to specified geographical areas, maximum power, or such other operating conditions, contained in this part or in the station authorization.

(c) *Safety/public safety priority.* The following access priority governs all DSRCS operations:

(1) Communications involving the safety of life have access priority over all other DSRCS communications;

(2) Subject to a control channel priority system management strategy (see ASTM E2213-03 DSRC Standard at §4.1.1.2(4)), DSRCS communications involving public safety have access priority over all other DSRC communications not listed in paragraph (c)(1) of this section. On-Board Units (OBUs) operated by state or local governmental entities are presumptively engaged in public safety priority communications.

(d) *Non-priority communications.* DSRCS communications not listed in paragraph (c) of this section, are non-priority communications. If a dispute arises concerning non-priority DSRCS-OBU communications with Roadside Units (RSUs), the provisions of §90.377(e) and (f) of this chapter will apply. Disputes concerning non-priority DSRCS-OBU communications not associated with RSUs are governed by paragraph (b) of this section.

[71 FR 52750, Sept. 7, 2006]

Reference:

http://www.ecfr.gov/cgi-bin/text-idx?SID=08e0eedb66c207cc0980be258cf48308&node=47:5.0.1.1.5&rgn=div5